Three Cheers for Unbreakable *Dolls*
True Stories of Amazing Pioneer Women in Arizona

Julie McDonald

The stories in this book are true. These stories were gathered from descendants, oral histories, books and articles. Research at fine pioneer museums throughout Arizona supplemented them. They represent history as seen through the eyes of the people who lived it. This book is meant to inform, inspire, and entertain. It is not intended to be used as a textbook of absolute fact.

Verner Gustav "Spud" Benson was born in Flagstaff, July 1, 1914. From a very young age he entertained family and friends with his cartoons. Whether at home, school or work (City of Flagstaff and Northern Arizona University) the cartoons brightened everyone's day! Over time he published hundreds of cartoons in numerous magazines, newspapers and periodicals. In the mid-sixties he ventured into a new arena writing dozens of humorous short stories about life in Flagstaff and Northern Arizona in "the good old days." He had many fans around the state and country but I was always his biggest fan! He was a gifted artist and writer but more importantly he was a wonderful father. He died over 30 years ago in 1981. I still miss him. I joined each profile of these amazing women with one of my dad's stories that complements theirs.

ISBN 978-0-9858952-1-1

Photos
Front cover: Cecil Cresswell, Circa 1929, Courtesy of the archives of the Old Trails Museum/Winslow Historical Society, www.oldtrailsmuseum.org

Published by Julie McDonald, First Edition 2013
Printed by Alexander's, Lindon, UT

© Julie McDonald
All rights reserved. Any reproduction of the contents by permission of author only. Please contact unbreakabledolls@gmail.com for comments, suggestions, ideas and corrections.

*To all my friends in Women's Missionary Fellowship
and their long suffering husbands.*

*Thanks for all the excitement, adventure,
and FUN we have had raising money for missions!*

*Having hundreds of garage sales, bake sales and craft sales.
Sorting buttons and jewelry till our eyes glazed over.
Selling gold teeth, vintage clothing, vegetables, rocks, peacock
feathers and things we found in the trash.*

*Ron and Charlene Talbott
Lou and Cathy Arminio
Randy and Linda Smith
Dave and Jane Scott
Daniel and Jennifer Witt
Gary and Elaine Barsness
Cliff and Cathy Lewis
Dave and Allison Kelley-Schaubert
Myron and Diana Leppke
Randal and Laura Ball
Mike and Lynn Gulvin
Bob and Vicki Goodwin
Lynne Gross
Faye Willis
Lola Montoya*

*To those who have gone ahead,
Jane Slusher
Owen and Marilyn Seumptewa*

Contents

Introduction		6
Map		7
Chapter 1	Sarah Ashurst	8
	Those Gamblin' Men	20
Chapter 2	Kate Lyall	23
	Hoboes and Tramps	29
Chapter 3	Martha Purtymun	31
	A Little More Police Brutality	40
Chapter 4	Guadalupe Vasquez	43
	The Clothes We Wore	51
Chapter 5	Cecil Creswell	54
	The Rumble Seat	62
Chapter 6	Katherine Beard	64
Acknowledgements		79

Introduction

Selling vegetables in my driveway at my farmstand has brought me fame, but not necessarily fortune. This feat in Flagstaff, Arizona, with its challenging growing conditions inspired my first book, "Farm Your Front Yard". I began the book with a brief synopsis of my grandmother, Mathilda Benson, a Swedish immigrant who came to Flagstaff in 1909. She has always inspired me. She was widowed when my father, Verner Benson, was only two years old. She raised all six children alone and put them through college selling vegetables that she grew on a little half-block farm in downtown Flagstaff. I was so happy that many of my readers found her story interesting. I wanted to write more about her, but her story is not enough for a whole book. As I thought about it, I began to wonder if there weren't other women like her, who had not been written about before. Not the rich and famous, which really lived much easier lives, but other immigrants, minorities, those that worked hard, faced impossible difficulties, experienced one setback after another, yet remained "Unbreakable". These women are the true unsung heroines of the West.

My first book "Unbreakable Dolls" has my grandmother's story along with seven other ordinary yet amazing women from Northern Arizona. With each story I included one of my dad's wonderful short stories about early days in Arizona which were published in the 1960's -70's. "Unbreakable Dolls, Too" has six more wonderful stories of amazing women paired with complimentary stories of my dad's. I began working on "Three Cheers for Unbreakable Dolls" even as I was finishing "Unbreakable Dolls, Too".

In the course of my research I have found the most fascinating stories that don't fit the Unbreakable Dolls profile: men, bad women, and even some animals. "Colorful Characters: Saints and Scoundrels of the American West" will be my next book.

For now, be inspired, encouraged and challenged by six more Unbreakable Dolls. Enjoy these women and my dad's fun stories!
—Julie

Significant Places Found in These Stories

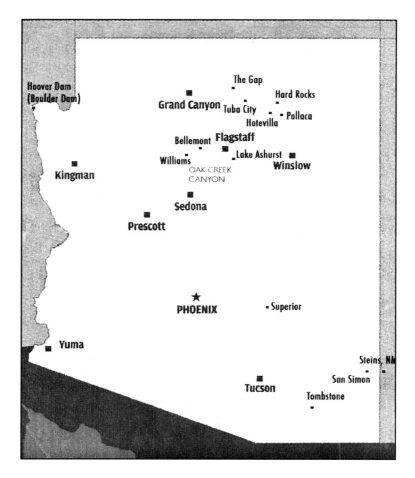

Note to the Reader:

The word, "Indian" is used in several of the stories. Today, this is considered outdated even offensive. Instead we now name the tribe, Navajo, Hopi, Zuni, etc. or use the term "Native American". However, to be true to the cultural context of the era and to keep the original quotes in context, I use the word "Indian" as it was written.

Chapter One

Ashurst
1854-1924

Sarah poked absent mindedly at the small campfire. It was warm now in the daytime but the September nights were chilly in the high desert of Northern Nevada. She wanted to keep the fire going should her husband Bill bring back some game to cook. Sarah anxiously watched the horizon for any sign of him. Bill had left early that morning in an effort to find game and/or any promising ore deposits. At nine months pregnant Sarah was hoping his excursion would not be a long one. She had been having contractions for several hours and they were getting much closer and stronger. Where was Bill? Sarah watched her two year old daughter playing quietly. Eve was still sleepy after waking up from her nap but soon the energetic little girl would be all over the camp.

As Sarah paced back and forth she wondered how she had come to be in such a predicament. Both Bill and Sarah had come with their families from Missouri during the California Gold Rush which began in 1849. Shortly after arriving in California, both of Sarah's parents died leaving Sarah, her sister Lydia and brother Andrew orphans. Andrew was 15 and deemed old enough to take care of himself, but the two girls were only 5 and 7. Sarah and Lydia were taken in by family friends, John and Lydie Borland. Sarah earned her keep by caring for the Borland's younger children. Sarah had met and married Bill when she was barely 16 and he was 26. Bill, always anxious for adventure had set his sight first on Nevada and then the Arizona Territory. It was slow going traveling in an uncovered wagon with a toddler and a herd of sheep. They hoped to journey on toward Arizona before winter set in.

As the sun sank lower in the western sky, Sarah was nearly

Sarah Ashurst as a young girl. Photo courtesy of the Ashurst Family.

frantic. She knew the birth was imminent and with no sign of Bill she feared she would give birth alone. What was she going to do with little Eve? She couldn't be left unsupervised; she could fall in the fire or wander off. The desert was full of dangers including wild animals and poisonous snakes. With no other options, Sarah took Eve by the hand, tied a rope around her wrist, and then tied the other end to the wagon wheel. Sarah gathered the things she would need and went into a tent where she gave birth unassisted. Bill finally arrived back at the camp and presented Sarah with one small rabbit. Sarah presented Bill with one small baby boy whom they named Henry Fountain Ashurst.

It took the little family two years to move from Northern California, through Nevada to Arizona with their herd of sheep. They crossed the mighty, untamed and treacherous Colorado River at Stone's Ferry, near the site of present day Hoover Dam. In 1875 the family first homesteaded near Williams. Sarah recalled their time there, "Our nearest neighbors were the Pittman's, 14 miles away. They were a wonderful family." Their home was nothing more than a hut. On Christmas Day of 1876 Sarah gave birth to another son, William. That same year people and animals were devastated by a terrible drought. Bill began a search for land with a more permanent source of water. After exploring the area, Bill found a beautiful spot close to a natural lake, with an abundance of natural springs and open meadows. It was in the forest of ponderosa pines, close to the rim. The herd could be driven down to a lower elevation should there be heavy snow. Bill and Sarah, now with three children said goodbye to friends and began the trek to start all over on a new homestead. Bill had indeed found a beautiful piece of land! A large outcropping of huge malapais boulders protected it from wind. There was a large open meadow, perfect for grazing animals and a garden. A large lake, which would be eventually named Lake Ashurst in the families honor, was not too far away. A cool clear spring bubbled out from beneath the rocks. Cattails grew near the spring, evidence it would be permanent. Water or the lack thereof could make or break a homestead in Arizona.

Bill began work on the cabin and outbuildings. What Sarah wanted more than anything was a cook stove! For eight years, Sarah had cooked 3 meals a day, every day over a campfire or at a fireplace. A stove was purchased from a company in San Francisco for $105.00. It took three months to get to Arizona. It was loaded on a ship and went from San Francisco, around Baja California. It was then loaded on to a steamer, which went up the Colorado River to Ehrenberg. From there it was freighted by bull team 140 miles to Prescott. Upon its arrival there, Bill hitched up his team of horses and drove his wagon to Prescott where the precious cargo was picked up. The freight charges were 100.00. Sarah was overjoyed when it finally arrived!

For five years the family lived year round at the homestead, meeting the requirements to "prove up." Upon completion of the cabin and outhouse, a barn for milk cows and horses was built. A bunk house for the hired cowboys was built. There was also a chicken house, root cellar and shed. Sarah kept a large productive garden. She milked the cows, cared for the chickens and an occasional pig. She cured all the meat. She made soap out of animal fat and lye. During the summer she made candles so the family would have light in the evenings during the long dark winters. She made moccasins out of deer hides or other animal skins for the whole family. She made garments for her growing in size and growing in number of children. She weaved by hand straw hats from reeds she found growing in the area to protect the family from the summer sun. She used the root cellar for her preserves and vegetables. She kept a crock of milk and butter in the cold water of the spring. She doctored injured and wounded men, including their many ranch hands, and nursed sick children. She continued cooking three meals a day, every day for her family and any hired hands that were living at the ranch. During this time another son, Thomas was born in 1880.

Two major events which occurred while the family was living year round at the homestead would never be forgotten. One morning Bill left early to go to Flagstaff for supplies. Sarah was out working in the garden, the children were doing chores. Sarah looked up and was terrified to see Indians riding swiftly toward the cabin. Most interactions between homesteaders and natives were positive but the times that turned deadly had left both sides fearful and suspicious. Rumors had been circulating the last few weeks that a band of marauding Indians had been terrorizing homesteaders in Northern Arizona. Sarah grabbed all her children and ran to the rocks where they huddled for hours in a cave. Where was Bill? Sarah did everything to calm her frightened children, she prayed, sang softly to them, quoted scripture. Finally the Indians left with no major damage done.

The other event took place in the snowy winter of 1881-1882. The family had been blessed with another girl, much to Eve's delight after three brothers! Just two weeks before her first birthday, little Margret became ill. Everything that could be done was done but little Margret succumbed, dying on the large flat rocks in front of fireplace where she had been born less than a year earlier. Bill made a tiny coffin while Sarah made the grave clothes and carved a rose out of wax to adorn the coffin. The snow was too deep for a burial so Margret was kept in the shed. When there was finally a break in the weather, and the ground thawed, the family trudged out to a burial site for the service. A large granite tombstone was placed over her grave which remains to this day.

In 1882 another baby was born who they named Charles Commodore. That summer Bill sold all his sheep and purchased 400 head of cattle from Henry Wingfield of Camp Verde. When asked about this surprising turn of events great grandson Everett Ashurst explained, "My great grandfather was not a sheep man, or a cattle man or a miner or a prospector. He was an "opportunist." I guess you would call him an "investor" today. He looked for opportunities and the potential for something to become profitable."

Bill and Sarah had received little in the way of education and they wanted it desperately for their children. Their son, Henry Fountain Ashurst, Arizona's first senator, described them this way in his diary, *A Many Colored Toga*. Entry dated October 2, 1914, "My parents were wholly uneducated. My father was of English ancestry and had mental strength; my mother was of French-Dutch ancestry, of courage and first rate intellect. They employed tutors to come to the ranch to teach. Our first tutor was Mr. Harry Fulton, a cultured man from Baltimore; our next tutor was an erudite Irishman named Joseph H. Terry who, at the ranch, went insane during a recitation hour and years later died in an asylum. Our third tutor was an Englishman named Wauemphast who wore burnsides and a salt and pepper suit, but my father objected to his cockney accent, discharged him and moved our family to Flagstaff when the public school opened in 1883"

When Bill and Sarah heard that a school would be opening in Flagstaff, Bill loaded up his three oldest, Eva, Henry and Billie and took them to Flagstaff. There were a total of seven children enrolled in the school. Eva Marshall (Marshall Elementary School) was the first teacher. The school met in an abandoned 10x20 tie-cutters cabin. The door had to be kept open for light as there was only one small window. The entire family moved to Flagstaff as soon as a house could be obtained. They purchased a home on Aspen street with a nice front porch that faced south and took advantage of the winter sun. The house stood where the current Flagstaff Public Library is now located.

Platt Cline writes in his book, *They Came to the Mountain*, "After a short amount of time, the teacher, Mrs. Marshall complained that 'It is impossible to teach with the promiscuous pistol shooting coming the saloons in Old Town which interfere with class work.' After a month the board procured a log house on the south side of Flagstaff , some distance from the saloons and the pistol play." Money for the teacher salary was scarce and

Bill Ashurst was often the source of pay, either personally funding the school or "passing the hat." From that time on the family stayed in Flagstaff in the winter and only spent the summers on the Ashurst Ranch, as it was called. Sarah would plant her huge garden, and the men would work the cattle. More and more of Bill's time was devoted to his mining ventures.

The family continued to grow in size and in number, Charles Commodore was the last to be born at the ranch in 1882, while in Flagstaff, Andrew, Edward and Maude Myrtle were born. All the children excelled in school. Henry had been noted practicing in his primer the title, Henry Fountain Ashurst, United States Senator. After graduation, he began pursuing a law degree. He also had a flare for public speaking. He practiced his speaking on cattle, horses and cactus as he worked side jobs as a cowboy. He also practiced on the 50 or so prisoners he was responsible for at his job of turn key, in the county jail. In 1897 Henry received a bible from his mother. Great-grandson Everett Ashurst has been entrusted with the care of his great uncles well-worn Bible. He read to me the inscription inside,

> March 28, 1897. For good conduct in the 19th legislature of the Arizona Territory.
> Henry,
> When far away from home and Mother, and temptations around you hover, turn to Matthew 6.
> -Mother

Then Everett in his cowboy drawl quipped, "Don't you just wish the lawmakers in Washington today would be reading Matthew Chapter 6 on a regular basis?"

Eva graduated high school and married Albert Pitts. They moved to a ranch near Ash Fork. In 1894, Bill and Sarah's youngest daughter Maude Myrtle was only one year old when they had their first grandchild, Albert Pitts, Jr. William, Thomas, Charles and Andrew were all graduating or near graduation from high school.

With the older boys busy with school and jobs, Bill often took his youngest son Edward on his adventures. Edward, born in 1890 was an agreeable child to have around and loved the time with his father. All the children addressed their parents throughout their lives as "Father" and "Mother".

One summer day in the late 1800's Bill went into town to get supplies. He took Edward with him. They did not return. Sarah was worried, not about Bill but the welfare of her young son. What possibly could have detained him? As Sarah had asked so many times in her marriage, "Where was Bill?" Finally she spotted the wagon coming down the dirt track. Bill, in his own mind had good news. He knew his wife might not see it that way. He had been practicing all the way home, hoping a good presentation might impress her. "Sarah", he said, "I have good news! A wonderful thing has happened to our family. While in Flagstaff, I had an opportunity to participate in a poker game. I won 10,000 dollars in gold coins!" Sarah was not impressed. Sarah was furious! "Bill Ashurst, you just as easily could have lost everything we have worked for! The ranch, the house in Flagstaff, everything. That money is ill gotten gain. You will NOT bring that filthy lucre into this house!" Defeated, Bill took his winnings and trudged off to the barn. The next day he rode off on his horse and with his 10,000 poker win and buried it on the homestead, telling no one where it was.

For several years, Bill, now in his mid-fifties, had been dreaming of moving to Australia. Such wonderful stories he had heard! Now with 10,000.00 this dream could become a reality. Sarah had no intention of moving to Australia. This became a serious source of friction between them and in 1898 they quietly divorced. Sarah deeded

---

The $10,000.00 Poker Win
How big was that poker win? Although no one today would scoff at $10,000.00, it doesn't seem like a life changing event. But how about in the 1890's. I asked my friend, Randon Cupp, who works for Chase Bank. He investigated and found that $10,000 then would be equivalent to $270,000! The win was in gold coin, what would that be worth? For that information I asked Michael Higdon owner of American Bullion and Coin here in Flagstaff. He said, "The coins would most likely have been $20.00 gold pieces. There would have been 500 of them. Today that would be worth $887,500!" Now add one other factor, land was dirt cheap in Arizona in 1890's. The Ashurst family could have bought most of Flagstaff, certainly all of Sedona with Oak Creek Canyon thrown in too boot. This puts Sarah Ashurst's moral resolve at a whole new level!

the ranch to Bill and he deeded the house on Aspen Street to her. Great grandson Everett Ashurst explained, "For my great grandfather, life was one big party. My great grandmother never forgot the frugality necessary for survival as an orphan. Her life was, "work hard and keep your nose to the grindstone." Bill sold his cattle and decided to spend one last winter working his mines in the Grand Canyon, and then he was off to a new life in Australia!

In February of 1901, John Hance, Bill's mining partner from the Grand Canyon arrived in Flagstaff with bad news. Bill Ashurst was dead. Bill and John had arranged a meeting at John's home on the rim of the Grand Canyon on February 1. Bill was always punctual and when he didn't arrive for the scheduled meeting, John was worried. John headed down the trail to the base camp of the Arkansas Mine and came upon the body of his friend. Bill Ashurst was lying on his back with his hat placed firmly over his face. Apparently a rock slide had come down where Bill had been gathering wood for a fire. Bill's legs had been pinned beneath a large boulder. Unable to free himself, he had died a slow agonizing death. He was meticulous in keeping a diary and the last entry at the camp was January 17, 1901. He did have a piece of paper and pencil on his person, writing his last thoughts and his sad state. As the end neared, the writing became unintelligible. He wrote about many things, but not the location of his 10,000 poker win. John Hance, other friends and three of Bill's sons, Henry, Charles and Andrew made the long trip to the Canyon and then the treacherous hike to the bottom near the Colorado River to recover the body. However, the condition of the body made it impossible to move. They walled the body with rocks to protect it from animals. It would be 10 years before the skeleton could be removed to the rim. In 1936, the family moved the remains again to the Pioneer Cemetery in Grand Canyon Village.

More than a few people made the 25 mile trip from Flagstaff to the Ashurst Ranch hoping to find the buried treasure. The ranch was literally filled with holes. One of the Ashurst ranch hands offered to stay at the cabin as a "caretaker". After a couple of months he packed up rather suddenly and moved to Idaho. He returned two years later, a wealthy man. In telling the story Everett added, "The family wasn't bitter, it was stated as a matter of fact that he had probably found the $10,000."

The family suffered another blow in September of that year when Thomas, only 20 years old died. He had been living with Eva and her family in Azusa, California. Eva died in Azusa in 1905.

The older boys were now on their own. Sarah's plan after Bill had gone to Australia was to take in boarders. She now put her plan into action. Sarah, Edward and Maude moved from Flagstaff to Azusa, California, where she had family and it was warmer. She purchased a home and supported herself the remainder of her life by taking in boarders.

Henry Fountain Ashurst, Arizona's first Senator. Photo courtesy of the Ashurst Family.

On September 27, 1918, Sarah suffered a double loss. She learned of the death of her sister Lydia, and her grandson, Albert Pitts was killed in action in World War 1.

She watched three sons, Henry, Charles and Edward become lawyers. William "Billie" was a teacher and principal, but also a successful rancher with a large spread near Young, Arizona. Andrew moved to Big Lake, Washington where he was involved in a variety of enterprises including ranching. Her son Henry became Arizona's first senator when Arizona became a state in 1912. He was known as "the silver tongued orator from Arizona" and served the state and country for nearly 30 years.

Sarah traveled by train to visit with her children and grandchildren and they often came to visit her. In 1924 her health began to fail. Henry Fountain Ashurst describes her passing in his published diary, *A Many Colored Toga*:

April 12, 1924
"Telegram from my brother William advising that my mother is very ill. This is written on Pennsylvania train on my journey to Azusa, California."

April 16, 1924
"Each station into which my train draws fills me with alarm, fearful that I may receive telegram with dolorous news. Reaching Azusa, I entered Mother's house and found her alive and cheerful. My brother Edward and wife and son are here from Oregon; my brother Andrew is here from Big Lake, Washington State; my brother Billie is here from Arizona, and my sister Maude, worn by the long vigil, is here from Needles, California. Mother's house is bright and clean and has just been painted and has new wall paper."

April 17, 1924
"Arose at 5:00am and soon the great cathedral of outdoors was filled with feathered songsters, singing songs that meant a thousand things. Phoned to Los Angeles for heart specialist who came and said Mother will live some weeks."

Azusa, April 18, 1924
"Mother's only living brother, Andrew J. Bogard arrived from Goldfield, Nevada. He is seventy-eight years old, was a frontiersman, sometimes sheriff of Tehama County, and saw life's seamy side in the early California settlements. He is gentle and soft spoken. I have not seen him for twenty-nine years."

April 19, 1924
"Mother much better this morning. The old light returned to her eyes, and with that unfailing regard for other persons which was a rule of her life, she said to me: 'Go back at once to the Senate; your duty is there. You must not shirk; therefore return to Washington.' My brother Charles will arrive from Detroit this evening."

April 22, 1924.
"To LaSalle Hotel, Chicago, where the clerk handed me a telegram. After seating myself I opened it and read the stabbing news: Mother died 4:30 pm Sunday. Billie"

Henry Fountain Ashurst then writes this beautiful tribute to his mother:
"Thus ends the actions and words but not the influence of a brilliant, dauntless woman who constantly gave her strength for those who needed help and mercy. No one doubts the existence of an Infinite Power and I am content that a Divine Healing will recompense her for the distress and misery she encountered in her seventy stormy years here."

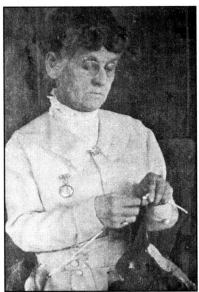

An older Sarah Ashurst. Photo courtesy of Ashurst Family.

Life facts:
William Henry Ashurst   1844-1901
Sarah Elizabeth Bogard Ashurst   May 1, 1854-April 20, 1924

Eve "Eva" Sept 8, 1872 - Jan 15, 1905
Henry Fountain   September 13, 1874- May 31, 1962
William "Billie"   1876-1956
Thomas Jasper   1880-1901
Margret   1881-1882
Charles Commodore   1882-1961
Andrew Jackson   1884-1960
Edward Bates   1890-1971
Maude Myrtle   1893-1973

Grandchildren: 11

Favorite recipe: Stew
Often heard Quote "Have you seen Bill?"

Gamblin' Men
They didn't win the West, but they won just about everything else
Verner G. Benson
June 1972

In the early 1900's, the roulette wheels in Arizona spun for the last time. The boys in the back room raked in the last chip and doors that had never been locked were closed with makeshift devices because the key had been thrown away when the place was opened. Legalized gambling was over. And people even talked darkly of women voting.

Professional gamblers may not have won the West but they, at one time or another, won just about everything else. There is a widely held belief that gamblers were hatched like chickens, falling in the evil companion on Friday, smoking Cubebs and playing Snooker on Saturday and then playing poker in a gilded den of sin with body snatchers on Sunday. They emerged Monday a full fledged gambler, complete with diamond stick pin.

Nothing could be further from the truth. Professional gamblers were exactly that, professionals. It was a hard profession calling for a variety of skills that took years to master. The novice must first learn to handle cards, fast and smooth. He must learn to calculate odds in seconds (gamblers were the first computers). He needed to know all the various means of cheating including marking cards with a pin imbedded in a ring and shaving cards – a delicate operation in which the edges of key cards were shaved microscopically. He must be able to spot confederated, casual onlookers with 20-20 vision, low morals and an elaborate system of signals. His knowledge of cheating was usually to protect himself from cheats. Good professional gamblers seldom cheated for a variety of reasons. It was unhealthy and discovery could bring a reprimand, possibly five of them, neatly wrapped in lead. It was impractical because a body could spend half the evening marking a deck and then have some idiot call for a fresh one. It was unnecessary because the pros had a thorough knowledge of each game and an uncanny ability to read faces. Playing against cattlemen with large spreads and short memories, cowboys whose condition enabled them to see four aces where only two existed and businessmen who believed in luck and drew two cards to fill an inside straight gave the gambler all the edge he needed.

As most of these players carried guns and quite often took umbrage at the gamblers' consistent winning, gamblers also carried guns. They were guns, not toys. The small caliber derringer might suit the Mississippi gambler but here the disenchanted were carrying .45s with a built-in smoke screen and a kick of a mule. It was desirable to meet firepower with firepower.

The elegant clothes of the gambler did not fit in with holsters and cartridge belts but this presented no problem because the tailors were used to that sort of thing. Luke Short had his weapon, a .45 with a seven-inch barrel, cut down almost to the cylinder and a leather-lined pocket sewed into his trousers. No bulge marred his slender frame. Some gamblers merely tucked their weapons into their trousers, after first removing the front sight because it would have been embarrassing to remove a button with the sight during an altercation.

The heavier gun also had advantages because most gamblers preferred to tap a fellow player alongside the head rather than shoot him. The argument was thus settled amicably, the cards remained unsullied and the game was not interrupted by explanation. Willing hands were always nearby to carry the incumbent outside and lay him gently in the nearest horse trough. Shootings called for investigations and sometimes broke up the game for a half hour or more. Doc Holliday carried both a gun and a knife and used them quite freely. He would have preferred a sawed-off shotgun, his favorite weapon, but other players demurred at having it lying on the table.

It is sometimes difficult to remember that gambling during this period was not only a legal profession but an honored one. The gambler was king in a newly settled boomtown. His clothes were the best quality and the heavy gold watch and chain were almost a badge. Diamonds adorned his fingers and tie and his boots were handmade and glistened. He spoke softly and made every attempt to appear a gentleman, doffing his hard hat to ladies and even those who were not considered ladies, a mark of respect to another professional.

There were tinhorns, of course, a name derived from small-time gamblers who dropped dice into a horn-shaped tin device, crossed with wires. They were small-time stakes with local rubes. Few of them acquired the stake necessary for the really big games for they spent a great deal of their time traveling between towns at the request of various law enforcement agencies.

Most of the adult, male population of early Arizona gambled. There were no YMCAs or USOs. The saloon and gambling hall supplied entertainment. It was a profitable business. Most gold mines were not worth shucks alongside a first-rate saloon and gambling hall. It has been reported that, during the height of the boom in Tombstone, Wyatt Earp received a thousand dollars a week for keeping order in the Oriental Saloon. It has also been reported that he did not. Wyatt Earp was first of all a lawman, next a successful businessman. Gambling was a sideline. One the other hand Doc Holliday was by vocation a gambler and a good one. He was also a killer but his was secondary, possibly a hobby.

As the boom towns faded and more respectable citizens moved in the gambler receded from the scene. Gambling was still legal but the young boisterous population was growing older, gathering wives and children and other impediments. There were days when not a shot was fired. An unarmed citizen might wear a plug hat in perfect safety. The final legal blow was only a formality. The gamblers had shook out. Where did they go? Well, politicians are not hatched out overnight, either.

Chapter Two

Kate
Lyall
1856-1939

Kate Lyall, circa approximately 1900.
Photo courtesy of the Lyall Family.

Kate lay in her bed looking up at the ceiling. She listened to crickets chirping and an occasional hoot from an owl. She had opened a window and the sweet desert fragrance wafted across the room. She was too excited to sleep. Tomorrow morning she, her husband Joel and 2 year old Arch would be going to Tombstone, in the Arizona territory, a rough and tumble town. They had a full day planned, visiting friends along the way, shopping, and going to the small postal station to pick up any mail that might have arrived.

Joel and Kate had come to the Arizona Territory from California. Joel's parents, Ambrose and Martha Lyall had a large ranch near Soldiers Hole, where the current town of El Frieda is located. Joel was a competent rancher, but he needed to have time to play his fiddle; he loved playing and was always in demand for dances. Joel was known as a "dreamer" and a "schemer" with an aversion to work. At age 9 he had walked all the way from Missouri to California behind the family's covered wagon. Surely there was an easier life than that! He had married Kate when he was 30 and she was 20. Two young sons had died while they were still in California, Joel Jr. at 18 months and John at 11 months. Kate constantly worried about little Arch, terrified something might happen to him as well.

It wasn't long until another baby arrived. After little "Dude" was born, the family moved further east just south of the tiny town of Steins, in the Animas Valley. Steins was in the New Mexico Territory, but a stone's throw from the border of the Arizona Territory. They brought some of the Lyall family cattle with them and it was there Joel began building a herd of race horses. Two more children were added to the family. Todd in 1889 and at last a baby girl, Lila in 1890.

One morning a posse arrived at the ranch in hot pursuit of bank robbers. Kate was away from the house at the time. The posse began interrogating the two young children, Todd and Lila, only 5 and 6 at the time. They asked the children for food and fresh horses, the children didn't know what to do and told them their mother would be home soon. When Kate arrived home the children told her what happened and how the posse had treated them. This made Kate mad. She went to the door and called out to them, "A fine thing, you are nothing but a bunch of thieves, chasing a bunch of thieves! I know every damn one of you, and you are nothing but a bunch of thieves!" With her opinion of this particular posse stated, she gave them the food and fresh horses they had asked for.

In 1897 Kate and Joel sepa-

Joel Lyall.
Photo Courtesy of Lyall Family.

rated. Arch was 14, Dude, 11, Todd 8 and Lila 7. Joel returned to California, completely abandoning the family. It fell to Arch to make a living for the family. He got out and punched cows, broke horses, took odd jobs, anything he could find to help feed the family.

In the early 1900's Kate decide to take up cattle ranching. How hard could it be? Certainly the last number of years raising 4 children alone had prepared her for about anything. She had grown up in a ranch family. Kate was born in Eshom Valley, California, which had been named for her parents. The beautiful valley bordered what would become Sequoia National Park. Kate had explored a number of places for her ranch. She was interested in an area along the Butterfield Stage Coach trail just west of Steins in the Arizona Territory. The names of the landmarks along the trail were a bit disturbing. Doubtful Canyon, Doubtful Mountains, Doubtful Arroyo, Doubtful Valley, Doubtful Peak and Doubtful Boulder. When Kate inquired about the names, she was even more disturbed. It was named that by early settlers who were "doubtful" they would survive, she was told.

Kate bought land in the western end of Doubtful Canyon called The Narrows. Her home was a dugout, literally dug into the side of a hill. Along with her cows, she kept chickens, and planted a productive garden.

In 1910 the family was devastated by the sudden death of the youngest son, Todd, only 21. Todd had been conducting a mine tour for executives at the mine in Ray. There was a huge explosion and everyone was killed. The mine purchased the largest granite tombstone in the Steins cemetery. Some said in hopes Kate wouldn't sue the mine.

On a hot day in June in 1917 Kate was surprised to see a large touring car arrive at her home. Out stepped elegant Annie Giddings Brown from Texas. She had come to find the grave of her father, J.J. Giddings who had been killed by Apaches in 1861. Kate put her up for the night, fed her, and Arch helped her to find the grave. Annie Giddings Brown later wrote of her trip and raved over Kate's and Arch's hospitality to her, a complete stranger.

Another visitor from Texas was a city girl named Nellie Hill. Nellie would come to Steins to visit her half-brother, Baily Smith. Nellie had fine clothes, a business degree and a good job in Dallas. It was on one of those visits she met Arch Lyall. They were married a short time later. It was an adjustment for Nellie to move to Steins after her big-city life in Dallas.

A baby was born to Nellie and Arch and on their way home to their ranch, which was not far from Kate's, the horse drawn wagon lost the front wheels and newborn Clarence bounced right out of the wagon. Nellie was beside herself with fear. She cried all the way to Kate's, then handed her the tiny bundle. Kate unwrapped the baby and pronounced, "He's fine. Nothing wrong with this baby." In the following three years, Arch and Nellie had two stillborn babies. Much rejoicing accompanied the arrival of baby Donald in 1920.

A few months later there was another arrival, but there was no rejoicing. 23 years after his divorce from Kate, Joel Lyall was back on her doorstep. The years had taken their toll. Joel was in sad shape and blind. Tough but tenderhearted Kate took him in. Arch was not nearly as sympathetic. "Had no use for him" said Arch's son Clarence years later, "leaving the family and leaving a 14 year old to work and support them made for hard feelings." Joel didn't stay long. A short time later a letter arrived saying he had passed away.

Kate, baby Donald, Nellie, Clarence, Arch Lyall, 1920 at Little Doubtful Canyon, AZ. Photo courtesy of Lyall Family.

Grandchildren were coming at a rapid clip and Kate delighted in them! The grandchildren all loved to go to Grandma Kate's. "We went as often as we could" said one, another added, "She treated us royally, did anything for us, would cook up whatever we asked for." In remembering her another grandchild said, "Grandma was funny. She had a sixth sense about things. She would get up some mornings and say, 'Company's coming'. She would cook up a bunch of food and sure enough, someone would come along to eat it. She would tell us something was going to happen and we would look at each other and think, 'that's crazy, how could she know that?' Then it would happen!" As the grandchildren got older they repaid her for her kindness, helping around her little house, caring for animals or chopping wood. They always knew what they would get from their Grandma Kate for Christmas; a Bible story book.

One day the family came to visit and was astounded to see a platter overflowing with fried chicken. Kate was known for her delicious fried chicken and

Grandson Donald, in Kate's corral in Doubtful Canyon, circa 1922. Photo courtesy of Lyall family.

this was treat, but why so much at one time? Apparently the chickens got into Kate's garden. "I got so mad at those chickens; I just grabbed them and tore their heads off. Teach those chickens to stay out of my garden."

In 1928, at age 72, Kate decided to "retire" and sold her ranch. She informed everyone in the family, "Come get your cows!" Before the advent of Social Security, elderly parents relied on their children for their care. Kate lived with all of her children at one time or another but mostly with Arch and with her granddaughter Catherine who she helped raise. The money she made from the ranch ran out after a few years and the depression years were especially difficult. Not only for Kate and her family but for everyone. Kate recalled watching the trains go through Steins. "Sometimes 200-300 men could be seen atop the freight cars. Men going from town to town, hoping to find work." Kate's own sons and grandsons had enlisted in the CCC, the Civilian Conservation Corps to help make ends meet for their families.

Kate was strong but also very kind. She was known as a soft

touch by the hoboes and tramps riding the rails in and out of Steins. One day a hobo appeared at her door. Whining and complaining he told her he was so weak with hunger he didn't know if he would make it or not. Kate said, "You're so far gone, I'll just get my gun and shoot you." The hobo literally ran to the edge of the property and jumped over a fence. Kate still had her sixth sense!

Kate Lyall remained in good health until July 25, 1939. At age 83 she suffered a heart attack and died. Kate had become somewhat of a legend in the Steins and Doubtful canyon area. Loved by her children, adored by her grandchildren and respected by all.

Life Facts:

Joel Lyall January 31, 1847- 1922
Margaret Catheryn "Kate" Eshom Lyall December 24/25, 1856- July 25, 1939 (born on Christmas Eve or Christmas Day, her parents weren't sure, they were traveling)

Married February 7, 1877

Children:
Joel Ambrose 12/11/1877-6/29/1879
John Edwin 2/6/1880-1/22/1881
Elmer Archer "Arch" 11/9/1883-1946
Guy Jefferson "Dude" 12/16/1886-1954
Henry Hiram "Todd" 2/5/1889-2/6/1910
Delilah Frances "Lila" Olney 10/2/90-1956

Grandchildren 9

Favorite Recipe: Fried Chicken

Hoboes and Tramps
Verner G. Benson
Winter 1976

Hoboes and tramps have almost disappeared from our ken. You just think you've found one and, lo and behold, he either turns out to be a professor studying the left hind leg of a grasshopper on a government grant and just waiting for his stipend, or the scion of an eminent local family being paid a sizable allowance to stay away.

Mr. Webster defines a hobo as: (1.) A migratory worker, or (2.) A homeless and usually penniless vagrant. He's not nearly as nice to tramps, for he refers to them as: (1a.) A foot traveler (b.) A begging or thieving vagrant. This is really not fair. It's true that a tramp might lift a shirt off a clothesline, but he always meant to return it, waiting only for a chance to wash it, not wanting to return it dirty.

The rumors that tramps would steal chickens are also unfounded. Here, again, it is true that a tramp would hold a warmed board close to a chicken roost on a cool evening and an old hen, clucking gratefully, would step onto it and be carried away to entertainment and dinner. The hen was under no duress and stepped freely upon the board of her own free will.

It was difficult to tell tramps and hoboes apart. The consensus of experts is that attire was the best yardstick. Hoboes brought a flair to clothing that few tramps could match. Derby hat, though slightly battered, striped trousers with an odd jacket, and always filigree work at the cuffs, even spats, and the length of rope to replace the mundane and ordinary belt or suspenders gave them a distinctly continental look.

Our Arizona drew an unusually high type of tramp, for it was considered a winter watering place only surpassed by Florida and California. Fall was marked, not by high flying geese, but by low flying tramps, heading for warmth and hospitality of Phoenix and Tucson.

Tramps traveled singly, not due to a lack of gregariousness, but to the fact the ordinary housewife paid little heed to a single tramp, while the sight of two tramps would call for a visit to the police or to the occultist. Three tramps would, of course, be considered a bevy and the mayor and common council would be hailed before the tax payers.

Tramps would work, under extreme conditions, especially late in the season when hearts had turned cold and handouts were few, but I regret to report a tendency to pile the uncut wood into a pile and throw a few sticks of cut wood on top, giving the impression of arduous labor for a simple meal. They also broke ax handles, and most wives had learned that the most gentle of men became unreasonable autocrats when removing a broken handle form a stubborn ax head. It was better to supply the meal and keep peace.

Most tramps paid for their meals by giving lonely housewives a glimpse of the outside world – glittering cities, far vistas and always the dissertation of the government, which they always called 'guvment'. It was possible, by merely listening for half an hour, to learn exactly what was wrong with the guvment and not only what was wrong, but corrective measures to be taken.

One tramp I particularly remember was referred to, for years, as the bodcake tramp. He was, I believe, an authority on pancakes, and ate thirty-seven of them, apparently in an effort to clear his palate. He spoke of eating pancakes in the best houses in the land and, as a beau geste, condescended to grade my mother's pancakes. He gave her an 86, if I remember correctly. One point lower, and I am quite sure reprisals and the business end of a broom would have descended on his bald shining pate.

There was a wide belief, among housewives, that tramps marked symbols on fence posts – a certain symbol standing for "bad dog", another standing for "soft touch", and so forth. I've never seen these but to avoid disappointment to the local housewives we used to mark signs on their posts with yellow chalk. Not knowing whether the signs were good or bad, the wives would rush out and scrub them off. They were promptly replaced. Flagstaff had the cleanest gateposts in Arizona.

Chapter Three

#

Purtymun
1858-1951

Martha walked slowly through the mercantile in Saticoy, California, thoroughly enjoying all the sights, sounds and smells. She selected a few cooking items and carefully inventoried all the fabric before she chose enough to make a new dress. She wanted to savor every minute in town before she headed back home. She gently padded her mail, a letter from her aunt and at long last, one from her father. She was anxious to hear from her father but she had learned from experience it was best to read his letters in private. Martha, called "Mattie" was grateful her brother Jesse had accompanied her in the wagon to town. He had offered to drive her and then watch his namesake, two year old Jess and baby Emory while she got supplies.

Upon arriving back home Mattie put away her purchases, tended to the boys then sat down and pulled out her mail. Eagerly she began to read the letter from her father. Mattie had not finished the first paragraph when she dropped the letter to the floor and burst into tears. Her father was in jail, accused of murdering a Mexican sheepherder who was grazing his sheep on her father's land. Not for a minute did Mattie think he might be innocent. He was a big man, at 6'6" he towered over most men. He was strong and powerfully built, with a hot temper. A bad combination. Mattie adored her father. What was she going to do? What could she do? She had to do something! She got up and out of habit began making bread. It calmed her nerves and helped her think. Somewhere in the flour and the yeast, Mattie got an idea. It was crazy, but Mattie was desperate. She ran to the shed and found a small hacksaw and brought it into the house. She measured the saw against her cake tin. If the saw were taken apart...

The next morning Mattie began making the "special" birthday

cake for her father. The base of the saw was placed at the bottom of the pan; the screws were tucked into paper and dropped in the batter. The handle would go into the top layer. Mattie was careful with the frosting. This cake had to hold together! Adding extra sugar to the frosting would cause it to be hard as cement. She hoped it wouldn't be appealing to the sheriff or any of the guards. She certainly didn't want them taking samples! Carefully she wrapped it up and prepared for her second trip into town in two days. She told her husband Stephen of her plan. He had expressed his doubts, but knew better than to try to stop her. She didn't tell her brother Jesse, sweet and sensitive Jesse, so much like their mother would be traumatized. Plus, he wouldn't be a bit of help in her scheme to get her father out of jail.

As Mattie rode to town she thought of all they had been through together. Her father "Bear" had come to California during the gold rush. He found it was more profitable to feed hungry prospectors than to be one. He used his hunting skills to provide meat for the miners. He also tried his hand at homesteading and he raised horses. He had met and married beautiful Nancy Cline when he was 36 and she was only 14. Nancy had come with her family from Holland around the Horn of Africa to San Francisco. Their first baby John had died. They almost lost Jesse, age 2 and Mattie who was an infant when a band of marauding Indians kidnapped the children. When the Indians met Bear returning home on the trail the terrified Indians tossed the children into a cactus patch and took off! Bear and the children were brokenhearted when Nancy died in 1861 at age 18. When she died Jesse was 5 and Mattie 3. Unable to work and properly care for the children Bear took them to the Santa Clara Mission. They remained there until he could put enough money together to provide for them. The three of them had suffered much together and they were very close. Mattie knew they would always be close. With these memories and thoughts swirling through her head, Mattie breathed a silent prayer. She was more determined than ever to get her father out of jail.

Mattie arrived at the post office and did her best to look calm and serene. The clerk looked at the address in Sacramento and smirked, "Pa in jail again I see, what did he do this time?" Mattie felt her cheeks flame red, but she held her head up, put her shoulders back and said nothing. Mattie was trembling as she slowly headed home. Would it work? Only time would tell. Mattie carefully calculated how long it would take for her father to get the cake and if he was able to break out, how long it would take for him to get home.

Every day Mattie watched the trail. One evening she spotted the unmistakable gait of her father. Overjoyed, she ran to meet him crying all the way. He soon told her, "I've been told I need to get out of California." Bear did what many others had done who were running from the law. He made plans to move to the last frontier, the Arizona Territory.

The whole family decided to move as well. Mattie, Stephen the two boys and brother Jesse. Bear traveled near them but stayed off the beaten path only taking his evening meals with them when it was safe to do so. Stephen's last name was Prettyman, but with the move to Arizona, they changed their name to Purtymun.

Pump House Cabin. Photo courtesy of Sedona Heritage Museum.

Stephen and Mattie lived for some time in Pinal near present day Superior; there two more boys were added to the family, Albert Wesley in 1881 and George Stephen, in 1884. They moved from Pinal to Pump House Wash, present day Kachina Village, 8 miles south of the little cow town of Flagstaff to be closer to Bear and Jesse. Stephen found work cutting wood for the tie camps. Bear was looking for somewhere isolated. He had heard about a remote canyon south of Flagstaff. At that time only a few white men had gazed into Oak Creek Canyon. Some saw the magnificent beauty. Others saw the potential for good fishing in the stream below. Others imagined gardens, and productive orchards. But when Bear Howard looked into the great expanse of the canyon he thought to himself, "The law will NEVER find me here!"

Back LtoR: Emory, Uncle Jesse, Bear Howard. Front LtoR: Jessie, Martha holding Pearl, Stephen holding Charles, Albert, George, sitting- Daniel. Photo courtesy of Sedona Heritage Museum.

Bear built a cabin at the confluence of Oak Creek and West Fork. He hunted bear which he sold to individuals and eventually to Babbitt's grocery store in Flagstaff. He built a trail to the top of the rim. This trail was called the Howard trail for decades until it was re-named the Art Young trail for the foreman of the Civilian Conservation Corps. The trail came out on the rim at Barney Pasture. There Bear kept horses and cattle. Once on the rim he could visit Stephen and Mattie and now 6 healthy boys, with the addition of Daniel Aaron born in 1886 and Charles Smith, in 1888.

Mattie's brother Jesse built a cabin further south in Oak Creek where Garlands stands today. The original cabin is now part of the kitchen at the world famous Garland's Lodge. Jesse was noted for his gardens, particularly the wildflowers he had cultivated and which covered a great deal of his property. His nephew Elmer Purtymun who served as Justice of the Peace in Sedona described his uncle this way, "Uncle Jesse was a lifelong bachelor. A bachelor whose love was, heavens to Betsey, peacefully reserved for flowers." Jesse ordered Himalayan Blackberries from a seed catalog and was delighted at their success in the canyon. Hi-

Purtymun cabin in Oak Creek Canyon, still standing and in use today. Photo courtesy of Sedona Heritage Museum.

malayan blackberries can now be found all through Oak Creek Canyon, and all the way to Cornville, 30 miles to the south! Stephen and Mattie grew tired of life at the Pump House. The winters were miserably cold. They longed for a good garden and wanted to start an orchard. Most importantly they wanted to be closer to family. They moved their belongings to the rim and used "Indian drags" to slide the items down the steep slope. Indian drags are made by placing a blanket, tarp or canvas tied between two poles. This acts like a sled on dirt or rock and deposits the items, hopefully still intact, at the bottom of the slope. Stephen and Mattie and the boys homesteaded a property now known as Junipine. They built a cabin, the only remaining cabin still in use in the canyon. They planted an orchard, still visible and productive today, and gardens. Mattie had learned how to shoot from her father and killed game, including a few bears! Grandson Elmer Purtymun said of her, "Grandma wasn't one of your namby-pambies. She was a crack shot!" At long last after 6 boys, in 1891 a little girl was born, Josephine Mabel "Pearl".

There was only a handful of homesteading families at that time. They were close and helped each other. They pur-

Purtymans fishing. Photo courtesy of Sedona Heritage Museum.

School in Oak Creek Canyon, 1899. Photo courtesy of Sedona Heritage Museum.

chased enough supplies to last for months. The winters could be harsh and in the spring the water levels in Oak Creek would rise and they could be stranded for a very long time. Mail came twice a week by horseback, if you were lucky. A school was built in the late 1800's halfway between two of the families, the Thomas family and the Thompsons.

These pioneer families knew how to have fun! During the summer there was a dance almost every Saturday night. Several times through the year but especially on the 4th of July they would all gather at Bacon Rind Park for a week of camping, feasting, singing, dancing and fishing. The fishing at that time was incredible with Oak Creek brimming with native brown trout. It was not unusual to catch several dozen. Occasionally during these week long festivals, a wedding was held. At one midnight supper, 75 people were in attendance. People came from as far away as Jerome, Prescott and Flagstaff to join in the fun. The Purtymun family were talented musicians. Jess, son of Stephen and Mattie played the accordion at picnics and church services. Other members of the family could fiddle. The Purtymuns could sing as well.

The 1890's were difficult years for the family. In 1892 Bear tried his hand at marriage again with the widow, Elizabeth Ragsdale James, a member of another Oak Creek family. But Elizabeth "couldn't stand the

Charles Purtymun, Sr. WWI. Photo courtesy of Sedona Heritage Museum.

smelly hound dogs lying around the house" and the marriage didn't last. Another little girl was born to Stephen and Mattie but Ruby May lived less than one month. Another baby girl, Ida Bell, was born in 1895.

Purtymun's cave kitchen, 1912, note the inscription on the cave wall, "Our Cave Kitchen, 1912, Oak Canyon." Jess with his accordian. Photo courtesy of Sedona Heritage Museum.

Sometime later Mattie did something quite scandalous- she divorced Stephen for alcoholism. Mattie had grown tired of his drinking and all the problems associated with it. Stephen packed up his things and returned to California. With Mattie's 6 able bodied sons she was able to maintain the homestead. She married James Cook, a widow with 5 children. Most of Mattie's 8 were still with her. For a time, Jim and Mattie Cook, affectionately known to everyone as 'Grandpa and Grandma Cook' lived in Yeager Canyon between Jerome and Prescott. Jim was a cattle rancher with a large spread and a big two-story home which could accomodate both families. A windmill provided water for the family and the cattle.

Jess Purtymun. Photo courtesy of Sedona Heritage Museum.

Different members of the Purtymun family continued living in the cabin in Oak Creek. It was and is a magnificent building. A long front porch runs along the entire length of the cabin. A south facing bay window with a window seat was added in the 1930's along with two additional bedrooms.

Bear lived with Mattie on

and off until his death in 1910 at age 93 in Yeager Canyon. He remained in remarkably good health and had become a legend in the Arizona Territory. His grave and death certificate reads "Charles Smith Howard" Many believed that was his alias, but in fact that was his real name, Jefferson Jesse Howard was the alias. That also explains the name of one of his grandsons, Charles Smith Purtymun.

Mattie with son, Albert, his wife Clara and two of their children, Charley and Zola, circa 1940's. Photo courtesy of Sedona Heritage Museum.

Mattie and Stephen's son, Jess remained in Oak Creek Canyon. He was the supervisor for the new road through the canyon which was completed in 1914. In his spare time Jess ran a still, a trade he had probably learned from his father. "Bootlegger" campground is named for him. Jess and brother Albert Purtymun both married Thompson sisters, another prominent family in the canyon. Jessie married Lizzie and Albert married Clara. Albert and Clara cared for their bachelor uncle, Jesse, until he died in their home in Clemenceau, near Cottonwood, Arizona in 1923, at the age of 67. Stephen and Mattie's son Dan ran the Page Springs fish hatchery. Emory was in construction building many of the buildings in Sedona. Pearl married her step-brother, Jim Cook.

Mattie out lived both husbands and 3 of her children. After Jim Cook's death, she spent time living in Fresno, CA near her daughters, Pearl and Ida, who were both nurses. Mattie, once again, had a productive orchard which she pruned and harvested herself, canning and making preserves. She remained active and interested in her children, grandchildren and great-grandchildren. She was known to everyone as "Grandma Cook", Paul Thompson, grandson of J.J. Thompson, the first settler in Oak Creek said of her, "She was forceful, but everyone liked her."

She went on many campouts with her family, even in her later years. Many photos show her camping in Oak Creek Canyon. One memorable camping trip was during a winter at Castle Hot Springs, near the present day Lake Pleasant. Mattie was miserable because they were camping in a cave and it was making her claustrophobic.

Mattie lived an amazing life dying at the age of 93. The Purtymuns had been active in the Assembly of God Church. Her grandson, the Rev. Dick Russell officiated at her funeral at the Wayside Chapel in Sedona.

Although Stephen and Mattie were among the first Settlers in the canyon, their sons and daughters were their true legacy to the Sedona area. Most of the children stayed and made significant contributions to the new community.

Life facts
Stephen M. Purtymun October 1854, Marysville, died in Fresno, California February, 1929
James Cook 1856
Martha Ellen Howard   March 18, 1858 Hormitos, California died December, 1951 Sedona, Arizona

Emory Howard   May   1877-1947
Jessie Elmer   March   1879-1942
Albert Wesley   May   1881-1961
George Stephen   Feb   1884-1964
Daniel Aaron   May   1886-1975
Charles Smith   Oct   1888-1977
Josephine Mabel "Pearl"   May 1891-1967
Ruby May   March 4, 1893-March 30, 1893
Ida Bell   May   1895-1957

Children of James (Jim and Sadie) Cook:
James 1879
Jessie 1881
Effie 1883
Dolly 1885
Josephina 1894

A Little More Police Brutality Please
Verner G. Benson
November 1968

Recently I received a traffic citation. The patrolman was impeccably dressed, smooth, urbane, extremely polite. He even called me sir. Since very few people call me sir I could have been smug about it but I flubbed it by turning around to see who he was talking to.

Like most taxpayers I was, by turn, innocent, indignant, a close personal friend of the Chief and, if I hadn't been wearing ragged Levis, "Someone to Reckon With." He gave it to me anyway.

It was a full week before it finally soaked in that while I hadn't done it deliberately, I was trying to beat a yellow light and hadn't made it. Since then I have been extremely cautious of caution lights. He might have saved me from a first class wreck.

Had he just yelled at me to a little all of this would have soaked in in two minutes.

Policemen in Flagstaff used to yell a lot. It was much simpler being a policeman in those days and much simpler being a culprit too.

It was an accepted fact that if you hit a policeman he would hit you back and probably add the going rate of interest too. If a policeman told you to come along and you didn't show any interest he would load you in anyway. Police cars of that period had running boards and anyone who had both shins barked on a running board would find it, as the educators say, a very meaningful experience. It was so meaningful, in fact, that very few came back for seconds.

Even during that period there was, however, police harassment. Acquaintances of mine who now except for occasional lapses are solid citizens, used to enliven dull evenings by harassing the police.

Armed with a burlap bag containing broken glass and a small paper bag they would loiter in front of a large plate glass window looking as guilty as possible. Eventually the minion of the law would pass by and view them with suspicion.

As soon as he resumed his beat and turned the corner, one would blow up the paper bag and break it with a bang and the other would drop the sack of glass to the sidewalk, then let a few shards of glass trickle to the bottom of the sack. It was the first rate imitation of the sound of a broken window.

The law would rush back around the corner, planning scathing words and possible arrest, and find the window intact. There was, at that time at least, no ordinance prohibiting the carrying of either burlap or paper bags but neither was there one prohibiting policemen from chasing kids.

The police were unhampered by ruling or writs. No law tied their hands (or feet) and the extent of their pursuit was governed by only one thing, wind. If one caught kids he was permitted to yell at them and possibly even smite them. And the next day he would give up his life to defend them. In that respect, at least, the police haven't changed much from that day to this.

Police brutality raised its ugly head in those days too.The city council, feeling that Flagstaff had become quite cosmopolitan, employed a motorcycle policeman. It was not a happy decision. Only a few of the downtown streets were paved. All the others had a washboard subgrade and were covered with gravel approximately the size and shape of the ball bearings used in roller skates.

In vain the patrolman lurked near the paved area. The citizens were uncooperative and drove sedately on the paved streets and speeded in the outskirts. The patrolman moved his base of operations and regretted it. It was brutal.

The gravel, on which he skidded at every turn, would have been grounds enough (no pun intended) but the city council, in its enthusiasm, had outfitted him too. Riding britches, the type so loved by Army officers of that period, at a distance gave the impression that he was wearing a pair of matched feed sacks cut off at the knees.

A wind resistant jacket that acted in the same capacity as a spinnaker on a racing yacht and a cap that tended to blow down over his eyes caused him, at speeds over 20, to become a sort of rudderless sailboat adrift on a choppy sea. Chasing a speeder up Birch Street, any sudden shifts of wind could send him on an abrupt tack and leave him chasing a little old lady up Cherry, one block over.

Pursuit of little old ladies was not desired by any member of the police. In fact, confrontations with little old ladies was avoided at any cost. Little old ladies of that period were terrors. My own mother, rest her soul, once held the entire fire department at bay with a broom. The roof was on fire and someone had notified the fire department but hadn't bothered to notify her. They finally scratched out some kind of a written pass and got in and put out the fire. They mopped the entire house before they left, not under

duress. They were just that kind of guys.

Another little old lady of the period drove a Model A with great nerve and daring.  Adopting some of the mannerisms and dress of World War I pursuit pilots she wore a scarf streaming out behind her and flew low. Each trip to town, accompanied by an entourage of barking dogs, was a saga of near misses and miraculous escapes. New patrolmen stopped her, but only once. Her rebuttals were delivered in a low tone, with faultless inflections and had the same general effect as a spray of scalding water.

Police people liked were given nicknames. "Flannelfoot" and "Gumshoe" were favorites. Another was known as "Rube," and one college watchman became widely known as "Two guns and a Knife." There was talk of issuing his check under that name so that he might experience less difficulty in cashing it.

Looking back it was nice being able to judge by the loudness of the policeman's tone the seriousness of the offense.

Sometimes it seems that not only are a policeman's hands tied these days but his jaw too. I'd like to see them both unshackled. Things would be noisy for awhile but they would soon quiet down.

Chapter Four

Guadalupe
Vasquez
1896-1984

Zacatecas, Mexico, 1910

Fourteen year old Guadalupe stood quietly at her bedroom door. In the dim candle light she could barely make out the figures around the kitchen table. Her parents and other family members were talking about Pancho Villa and his latest raid. To some in Mexico, Pancho Villa was a folk hero, stealing from the rich and giving to the poor. Guadalupe was frightened by Pancho Villa. She closed her door and crawled into bed. She wanted to think of something more pleasant. Fortunately there was something much more pleasant and it was in the very near future. Tomorrow, the family would be traveling 75 miles away to the town of Aguascalientes to meet some real Spaniards. Guadalupe was not sure she had ever met one. Oh, of course she knew many whose ancestors had come from Spain, but none who were currently living in Spain. Would she be able to talk to them? Would the Spanish be so different they wouldn't be able to understand each other? What would they be wearing? What would they think of her family and how they were dressed? What would they think of her? With all these thoughts swirling through her head, Guadalupe finally fell asleep.

It seemed to take forever to get to Aguascalientes. The family stopped often, visiting friends and family along the way. Finally they arrived. It was an exciting time. A great meal was prepared and soon everyone was talking and visiting. There was a difference in the language but everyone seemed to be getting along just fine. Guadalupe may not have understood the language perfectly but she knew the teen-age boy, only one year her senior had taken an interest in her. Sometimes you don't need language to communicate! Tranquilino was so taken with the shy Guadalupe, who kept her eyes lowered whenever she spoke, that when his father returned to Spain, he didn't return with him. Tranquilino found work in the family business, a beef slaughterhouse. He then began to court Guadalupe.

When Tranquilino was 16 and Guadalupe 15 they were married. If Guadalupe had been frightened by Pancho Villa, Tranquilino was horrified. How could Pancho Villa with his "army" of 5,000 men be terrorizing the whole country, looting, burning villages to the ground and running wild? Where was the law? The Federales, Mexico's police, were every bit as bad, maybe worse than Pancho Villa. This was NOT the way things were done in Spain! The more Tranquilino thought about it, the more convinced he was that he needed to get his wife and now baby daughter Isabel out of Mexico.

Two things that had always fascinated Tranquilino were the lumber industry and the railroad. Just north of the border, state hood had been granted to the territories of Arizona and New Mexico. There was logging and railroads in both states but one particular town intrigued him. Flagstaff, Arizona was a small town along the railroad surrounded by a large, some said the biggest in the whole world, forest of Ponderosa pines. The family rode a short distance in the family wagon with their few belongings to say their good-byes to their family. They all knew they might not ever see one another again. The little family purchased tickets on the train for their trip to El Paso, Texas. There Tranquilino obtained a work permit and the family was processed to come into the United States. In El Paso, they met others fleeing Mexico. Tranquilino and Guadalupe were not disappointed when they arrived in Flagstaff. Tranquilino was a hard worker. He never had difficulty obtaining a job or keeping

Guadalupe and Tranquilino at Dupont St. Photo courtesy of Vasquez family.

a job. His first job was with the railroad. He then took a job cutting firewood for the Flagstaff Steam Plant which was located on Phoenix Avenue. Tranquilino insisted the family learn English. "If we live in this country, we're learning English. We're Americans now!" They purchased two acres south of the tracks at 120 South DuPont Street, close to the Normal School, now Northern Arizona University. Here they started a farm. They built a house and barn. They acquired seven Holstein cows and two bulls. They kept a couple dozen chickens which they used for meat and eggs. They also kept pigs, rabbits and goats. Guadalupe's granddaughter, Mary Vasquez-Powell spoke proudly of her, "My grandmother was a traditional homemaker. She was the first one up, and the last one to go to bed, seeing to the needs of her family. She made most of the clothing for the family. She made quilts that were beautiful for the beds and quilts that were more practical for use outside and in the trucks. She also did embroidery and every day she braided her girl's hair. For special occasions she would weave a bright red ribbon in the braid, tying a big bow at the end. Sometimes she would bring both braids around our head, like a wreath."

Children came at a rapid rate until there were 10 in all. Tranquilino and Guadalupe had enough love to bring into their home even more children who weren't their own. After the death of his mother, they adopted baby Paul. Friends of the Vasquez family fell into hard times so Cruz and Cecilio Trillo were adopted into the family. Now they were up to 13 healthy and very happy children.

When World War II started, they had five sons that were eligible for service. Guadalupe thought of taking her boys to Mexico, but Tranquilino would not hear of it, "We are Americans; we will fight for our country!" Guadalupe felt a little better when all five boys also insisted that they enlist. Five boys served in combat in the Pacific Arena and in Europe. Guadalupe spent most of World War II on her knees. All five sons returned home safely.

At the end of World War II, Tranquilino and two of his sons started their own logging business, Vasquez Brothers Logging

Company. Another son, Gregory joined them a few years later. This business would serve the family for over 40 years.

Other changes were in store for the Vasquez family. After World War II the city fathers in Flagstaff deemed the town too "sophisticated" to allow farming in the city limits. The logging equipment kept on the property was also banned. They had no intentions of giving up their animals and equipment. Their son Mario purchased acreage off Lake Mary Road and he and his family relocated there. Their home was nice but small. So, they added a second story.

Guadalupe milking her cows. Photo courtesy of Vasquez Family.

There was enough property for Tranquilino and Guadalupe to also relocate out of the city. So, they did. There they helped out with the farm animals and enjoyed living near their son, his wife and their grandchildren. Their original home in Flagstaff and the Lake Mary property remain in the family today.

Tranquilino and Guadalupe heard that the grocery stores in town were throwing away old or imperfect vegetables. "What a terrible waste." they said. Tranquilino went to each store and offered to pick up the vegetables at the end of each day. It didn't take the farm animals long to recognize the truck loaded with veggies. They would race back and forth in their pens stomping the ground. The cow's favorite was the big purple cabbages. The grandchildren still remember the cows munching contently with purple juice dripping all down their chest and legs.

It fell to Guadalupe to milk the cows. She didn't like getting swished with a cow's tail so before the milking began, she whipped out a scarf used just for that purpose and tied the cow's tail to one of its legs.

Grandchildren came at a rapid rate, so many in fact there were enough for two baseball teams. Small bleachers were erect-

The Vasquez family, back (LtoR) Margie, Mary, Paul, Greg, Mario, Henry (grandson, standing in for his father, Pete who had died in 1953), Polly. Front (LtoR), Theresa, Isabel, Guadalupe, Tranquilino, Vicky and Tranky. Photo courtesy of Vasquez Family.

ed on the field at the property at Lake Mary and Tranquilino and Guadalupe were the cheerleaders—for both teams.

The grandchildren played other games as well, running and playing all over the property. They could play with most of the animals but the piglets were off limits. They would hear their grandparents say, "Don't play with the piglets!" One spring the temptation to play with those cute little piglets overcame the children and they went into the pen and brought out a few of them. The sows did not object to the removal of the piglets. It was then the children learned why they were off limits! Once the piglets wriggled out of their arms, they were impossible to catch. After hours of chasing them, the baby pigs were finally rounded up again and all the children had learned a hard lesson. It seemed to the children that the sows had been watching and laughing at them the whole time.

All this playing and running made for lots of hungry children. Guadalupe had a simple and delicious solution. During the day she would cook 4-5 dozen tortillas. They were placed in a big white porcelain pot off the kitchen door. Children could run by at any time and pull out a fresh, warm tortilla. If a child wanted butter for the tortilla, they had to go inside to get it.

Another treat for the children was gathering nopales, pads of the prickly pear cactus. During the summer the grandchildren would come to spend the night. Early the next morning Guadalupe would be up and ready to go at 8 a.m. She wore one of her aprons with huge pockets and a scarf around her head. Guadalupe always wore a scarf. She felt it was disrespectful for a woman to have her head uncovered. The children would follow her along through the woods as she gathered the pads of the prickly pear. There was no end to the uses for the prickly pear pads. She used them in sauces, eggs, chorizo, jams and salads. She also used them to make Christmas decorations. She would pack a lunch and carry it in a sling. As the children ate their lunch, Guadalupe pulled out her big knife and scrapped the thorns off the cactus, taking them out of one pocket and when they were cleaned, putting them in another pocket. It was during this time that Guadalupe told the children ghost stories she had learned in Mexico. These weren't ordinary, run of the mill ghost stories. Guadalupe had mastered and worked these to perfection. Every word, every phrase, expressions, hand gestures and even sound effects added to the excitement of the story! During the day it was all thrilling to the grandchildren, but on more than one occasion one or another, would suffer nightmares during the night.

Julia and Mario Vasquez. Photo courtesy of the Vasquez Family.

The Vasquez Family was a part of Our Lady of Guadalupe Parish. Tranquilino had brought much of the rock used for the construction of the church. A stained glass window bears their name. The family participated in many Catholic traditions in their home with all the children given roles or responsibilities. Festivities always ended with a big feast enjoyed by friends and family. The family home had a chapel where an annual tradition was the praying

Guadalupe and Tranquilino on a trip back to Mexico. Photo courtesy of the Vasquez Family.

of a novena for nine days ending on the Fourth of July. The chapel had an organ where the family sang hymns during the novena. Another favorite family tradition was attending the Gran Jamaica. It was a Parish fund-raiser with many activities that everyone enjoyed. There was a carnival, craft booths, food, confetti eggs and many other lively games that people participated in and enjoyed. It was always held on a weekend in September, with about 200 people participating.

Tia Maria, Guadalupe's sister from Mexico arrived and lived for many years with the family. She was a tiny thing, and was a real character! She was witty, funny and lots of fun to be with. Her specialty was making corn tortillas from scratch. She would show the children her hands and say, "Look at this. I have made so many corn tortillas that I don't have handprints any more. Now the FBI won't be able to find me." The children were awed by this and it never occurred to them that the FBI would have no reason to be looking for their Tia Maria.

Tranquilino and Guadalupe encouraged education for their children and grandchildren. However, as they aged, they felt all they were doing was going to graduations. They were always amazed that one child could have so many graduations, 8th grade, high school, college, and masters. Their oldest grand-daughter, Mary Vasquez Powell remembers every graduation after high school they would say, "What! You're graduating, AGAIN?"

They also enjoyed going back to Aguascalientes, Mexico to visit old friends and family. When they left Mexico, they never expected they would be able to travel there again. They were always thrilled to go visit and thrilled to be able to return home.

Both Tranquilino and Guadalupe were able to stay in their own home until their deaths. Tranquilino died from complications with diabetes in 1979. Guadalupe was lost without him and began to decline. A couple of years later their daughter Vicky took a leave of absence from the convent to come and care for her mother full time. Guadalupe died in 1984, telling ghost stories to the very end.

Life Facts:
Tranquilino Vasquez, born in Spain, 1895-1979
Guadalupe Vasquez, born in Zacatecas, Mexico, 1896-1984

Married: 1912

Children:
Isabel: June 6, 1913--- May 22, 1996
Victoria (Vicky also Sister Guadalupe Vasquez): November 8, 1916---October 30, 2003
Pete: September 9, 1919---May 10, 1953
Paula: June 3, 1921---December 10, 2006
Cecilio Trillo (adopted): November 22, 1922 (Living)
Mario: January 19, 1923 (Living)
Cruz Trillo (adopted): February 12, 1920 (Don't know year of death)
Gregory: February 13, 1925---November 7, 2001
Paul: January 29, 1926---July 10, 1989
Mary Ellen: February 17, 1928---September 5, 2006
Margaret (Margie): February 23, 1930 (Living)
Twins: Tranquilino Jr. (Tranky): December 4, 1934---December 26, 2000 and Theresa (Terry): December 4, 1934 (Living)

Grandchildren: 35

Favorite recipe: Yeast bread, tortillas, oatmeal raisin cookies

Favorite flower: geraniums, especially bright red ones

Often heard quotes:
"Andale, mija! Andale, mijo!" Hurry up little girl! Hurry up little boy!
"Si Dios nos da licencia." See you tomorrow, if God allows.

The Clothes We Wore
Verner Benson
February 1972

Recently I had occasion to pull a neighbor's child from an icy pond. This was not great feat for the water was only about four inches deep. I could not help but notice, however, as I snatched him forth by the scruff of the neck, the excellent quality of his jacket. A light thing, waterproof and warm with a hood neatly rolled up in the collar. I couldn't help compare it with the clothes worn when I was a child.

It was a brutal age, when small boys wore short pants and older boys wore long ones, not reversed as it is today. Boys wore short pants until the age of 10 or 12 and the transition from short pants to long ones, although welcome, was trying experience, accompanied by a good many tiresome lectures from adults and cat calls from colleagues. These were not the cool, comfortable shorts worn by youngsters of today but drab, knee length, tight fitting little horrors, designed, no doubt, by a mad undertaker who hated children. Worn with these were long, black (in deference to the undertaker), cotton stockings. The stockings and the pants were at odds when new, and as the season wore on, became completely incompatible, and the ensuing rift revealed a stretch of skinny leg, burned red in the summer and blue with cold in the fall.

If you were lucky and had racy parents, it was sometimes possible to talk them into knickers. Knickers were not as short, were comfortably baggy, and fastened below the knee, helping to hold up the dreadful stockings.

Woe, however, to the urchin who unbuckled one of the legs on the knickers and let them hang loose. He became a marked child and was watched closely by both Sunday School superintendents and truant officers. Letting a knicker leg hang was considered, by many, to be the height of raffishness, leading, eventually to the smoking of grapevine, late hours and even hanging around the Gopher Hole, a local pool hall.

Kids' shoes were heavy and were what the catalogs called 'serviceable'. Being serviceable meant simply that the right foot could slip into the left shoe without noticeable friction. They also had copper or brass plates on the toes. These plates were a great help to shoe salesmen, for parents could be convinced the plates would protect the toes of the shoes during marble season. It was only later the parents discovered the kids had worn the leather out around the plates, and they were left high and dry, like a grounded barge. A great many of the shoes also had plates on the soles, metal, fastened at both heel and toe. One could never be sure if the noise was coming from passing kids or Flamenco dancers.

In the matter of shirts, poor kids fared much better than the rich ones.

The poor ones wore their father's, cut down, standard, with tails. The rich were decked out in what was known as a 'Party Waist' – a miserable thing, cut short and equipped at the bottom with button holes. These, in turn, were fastened to buttons, sewed inside the tops of the pants. It was a dreadful combination for the buttons could cut through rawhide in a matter of minutes. Someone gave me two of them and I still wake up nights cursing his memory.

The basic item of all children's clothing during the winter months was long underwear, a delight to put on during the first chilly days of fall and an even greater delight to take off in the spring.

When first put on, the underwear fit tightly and gave the appearance of tights. It was much used to play 'Robin Hood'.

As days passed, however, the underwear seemed to grow, becoming more voluminous with each passing hour. At the ankles, the legs of the underwear assumed a bell-bottomed appearance and soon it was necessary to wrap the excess around the legs to accommodate the dreadful stockings. As the growth continued, the underwear bulged over the top of the stocking, giving the appearance of an advanced case of Elephantitis. Not to be outdone, the arms of the underwear grew apace and soon drooped over the hands of the incumbent, collecting jam, peanut butter and whatever else was in season.

The buttoned type of long underwear was bad enough, but someone, may he smother in his own invention, brought out a buttonless type. These had plackets at the shoulders and slipped on. Mothers bought them by the gross, believing their winter would be freed from sewing buttons. These too, grew and much faster than the occupant, and soon the plackets spread, giving the union suit an off-shoulders look and the entire suit, obeying the law of gravity, sought to drop to the ground. It was embarrassing, making an end run and being tackled and brought to earth by the neckline of your own underwear. By spring the underwear had reached its full growth and could have fit the Cardiff Giant with room to spare.

The clothes of the day were bad enough, but they were often aided and abetted by my mother, who made her own. She was a confirmed non-conformist, never content to trod the beaten path. If she wanted a word, she would try for it in English, fail to find the right one and try Swedish, miss it there, and make up one of her own. She did the same thing with clothes. Not for her the patterns of the day but new, and untried, ideas. She came up with prizes.

Her trousers were not made with a standard fly but with a slit, backed up by a patch of the same material set behind it. I have always believed she stole the idea from the Trap Door Spider. This arrangement as all very well, but the patch always seemed to be out to lunch or visiting a friend and was never available when needed. I would prefer to draw a curtain over the embarrassments encountered.

Another idea, possibly the basis for the present-day panty girdle, was the 'Leave.' Both the word and the garment were her idea. This was a garment designed to be worn underneath the shirt, something like a vest turned backward. It had a vaguely clerical look about it. To this were attached garters, fastened with a safety pin. The garters wound their way downward finally grabbing the stocking at the top. The safety pins soon tore up the cloth on the leave and the garter let go, releasing the long stocking, which fell, garter attached, and tripped four or five people. I dutifully attached the garters each morning, removing them after rounding the first corner, and replaced them with inner-tube bands. They were more dependable.

I don't believe I've ever worn garters since. The memories were too painful and so were the inner-tube bands. Why couldn't they have invented balloon ties in my time?

Chapter Five

Olive Dove Juanita Gale Cecil Creswell
1901-1954

Olive Dove Zoast leaned against the wall of the building which was being warmed by the sun. The crude bench was warm too and it felt oh so good to sit down. Olive was new in town and her first priority was to find a job. Olive had been on her own since she was 14 years old. After her mother, a Sioux Indian had died, her life had become intolerable. In the small town of Olivet, South Dakota, she faced prejudice being a "half breed". Her German father was harsh and treated her like a slave. At age 14, she ran away from home. Olive was a girl of many talents. A natural with animals, especially horses, she could work as a ranch hand. She was also a competent cook, laundress, housekeeper and good with children.

As Olive sat on the bench thinking where she might first apply for a job and warming herself she began to listen to the chatter coming from the boardwalk. She was tucked out of sight but not out of hearing. She began to listen to two women engaged in a lively conversation.

"Well I never, Clara, your sister goin' to be a Harvey Girl. I think it sounds right scandalous."

"Oh May, shush yourself, it's perfectly proper. The girls live in dorms and are workin 10-12 hours a day; they don't have time to git into trouble. Sides, they got a lady chaperone to see to it that they are doin' what they supposed to. She'll have good food, a clean bed and be makin' enough money to go to the teachers college. 'Less a course she meets a cowboy or a railroad man."

Both women laughed and their voices trailed off as they moved along. Olive thought to herself, "Good food? A clean bed? Money?" Olive wasn't sure what a Harvey Girl was but she was sure going to find out! Olive discovered the closet Harvey House was in Winslow, Arizona. She made immediate plans to go there.

The Harvey Girls with a vendor outside the Winslow Harvey House, circa 1918, shortly after Cecil arrived in Arizona. Cecil is the third from right. Photo courtesy of the archives of the Old Trails Museum/Winslow Historical Society, www.oldtrailsmuseum.org

The fact that Olive didn't meet the qualifications to be a Harvey Girl didn't stop her. She was not 18, only 17. She didn't have an eighth grade education; actually she had very little education. But she could read and write and do some arithmetic. Along with re-inventing herself she choose a new name. Juanita Gale had a nice ring to it.

Juanita loved her new job at the Winslow Harvey House. Most girls chaffed at the uniforms but Juanita loved having something fresh and clean and laundered for her. She quickly learned her job working with the other girls to get an elegant meal served to the rail passengers. Some of the girls complained about the hard work and long hours, but Juanita had never had it so easy. Whenever she had any free time, Juanita exchanged her Harvey Girl uniform for western wear and headed off to the Hashkife Ranch. Mack Hughes, a cowboy with the ranch remembered her and said, "She would come down to our barn and try to get us to let her ride one of our horses. She was a pretty good rider."

Many of the Harvey Girls met and married, Juanita was no exception. She married a local man but he was soon sent to prison for bigamy and Juanita returned to the Harvey House.

It wasn't long before another one of the local young men took an interest in her. George Creswell came often to sit at her station. He always showed up when it was slow between trains. The girls were forbidden to fraternize with the customers. Young men and women have been breaking that rule since there were young men and women! George would talk as much as he could to Juanita then slip her a note he had written earlier. In this way they got to know each other. Juanita soon took the plunge again and married George. With the change of her last name, she also changed her first name again- this time to Cecil.

George had a good job as a livestock inspector with the Bureau of Indian Affairs. They lived in Tuba City and also near Old Orabi. Being half Sioux, Cecil was very comfortable among the native population. The 1930 census shows George and Cecil as the only whites among all their native neighbors. Friends recalled that she was friendly, outgoing and knew everyone. One of her favorite activities was going to dances. Cecil and George often made trips back to Winslow to visit George's extended family and do some shopping. Casey's Hardware sold anything you might need. It was so well stocked people from Phoenix would come to shop there.

George and Cecil had a loving, happy marriage. Five days before Christmas in 1936, Cecil's world came crashing down. Her beloved George died suddenly sending Cecil into a downward spiral. In financial straits, Cecil married a man by the name of "Moon" Mullens. He was struck by lightning while riding the range near Lords-

Cecil Creswell, circa 1929. Photo courtesy of the archives of the Old Trails Museum/Winslow Historical Society, www.oldtrailsmuseum.org

> Cattle rustling was one of the big crimes of the 1800's. Cattle were a means of livelihood and their loss could spell disaster for entire families. Cattle rustling was immediately punishable by hanging. The cattle were "rustled" or stolen primarily by changing the brand. Calves were and still are branded at a young age by using the owners brand forged into a piece of iron. This was then placed in a camp fire until red hot then the calves hide was seared with this permanent mark of ownership. In the Old West it was not uncommon to see a calf with one brand nursing from a cow with another brand. The brands were changed with the use of a running iron. This was used only for changing of brands and to be in possession of one could result in hanging. They had no honest purpose. I love the quote from author Don Dedera, "Cowboys might be illiterate, but they could write the United States Constitution on the side of a cow with a running iron."

burg, New Mexico. Two other disastrous relationships took a heavy toll on Cecil. Heartbroken and without money Cecil moved back to Winslow. George had a homestead 6 miles south of Winslow. Mary May Baily explained, "You've got to remember that in those days a single woman didn't have much choice. Careers were few. If you had an education you became a school teacher or worked as a secretary. If you didn't, and Cecil didn't, you took in boarders or did washing or made pies." In addition, the Great Depression had put a chill on the nation and rural towns like Winslow were hard hit. There was no welfare, no food stamps, no shelters or Medicaid and no social security.

Cecil set about trying to make it on her homestead, all that she had. At 5'4" and 120 pounds she performed back breaking work. She mixed cement and river sand for the concrete floor and porch, laid the red sandstone walls for part of the house and plastered walls for the rest. There was never electricity, running water, or indoor plumbing. She read her books at night with the light of a Coleman lantern. She engineered a complicated gutter system to catch precious rain water. She tried to dig a well near her home, but failed to reach water. She had to carry water from Clear Creek, 1/2 mile away.

After her house was finished, she built a chicken coop. She

Cecil (right) and her friend Polyanna visiting from out of state, circa 1929. Photo courtesy of the archives of the Old Trails Museum/Winslow Historical Society, www.oldtrailsmuseum.org

built a 40 foot long wall with stones so heavy two men could hardly lift them. She built a 100x200 foot corral out of 8 foot mesquite limbs which she wired together.

Cecil, her ranch house complete ventured into a new career: Cattle Rustler. Cecil was the topic of conversation in every cowboy bar in the area! Mack Hughes, of Winslow, said, "Many in Winslow knew she was rustling cows, but it was considered for meat, rather than profit, and thus forgiven under the old tradition of the range." Her women friends were all in agreement in saying she was kind, gentle, friendly and feminine with a warm interest in children. "I first knew her when she was a Harvey Girl and later when she lived on her ranch. She was a good neighbor and a frequent guest in my home and always a perfect lady. She took an interest in my two small girls, two and three at the time and would play with them when she came to the house," said Iris Myers.

Being a woman, Cecil added some new twists to the old crime of cattle rustling. Once, needing a bull for her cows she rustled Tombo Kaufman's big light colored bull and herded him to her ranch. There she roped and threw the 800 pound animal to the ground branding him with her Rafter 3 brand. Then she took a bottle of Red Henna hair dye and proceeded to dye the entire bull a dark reddish brown so he would resemble the more common breed of Herefords. Kaufman, for a full year rode past Cecil's ranch, and his bull, and never recognized him.

Cecil's real love was horses, former deputy sheriff Jim Brisendine said. "She would go up in the mountains and catch wild mustangs and break them to ride. She broke wild horses the best cowboys in the country would shy away from. One of those was

Cecil and her beloved horse, Pig, 1929. Photo courtesy of the archives of the Old Trails Museum/Winslow Historical Society, www.oldtrailsmuseum.org

a huge black stallion she named "Pig", she had trapped, broke gentle and kept for her own. She always rode like a champion and treated her horse like it was a child." She would ride Pig into Winslow with some rustled beef and trade it at Babbitt's grocery store for supplies. Mary May Baily, added, "If she didn't have any beef she shot and butchered a burro. Burros were running free all over the range. Cecil would laugh about it when she told us."

One man who would not turn a blind eye to Cecil's rustling activities was her neighbor, John Thompson. What started as a property boundary dispute escalated into a feud which became legendary. Dale Hancock worked for Thompson as a youth. He recalled one of the many incidents, "Cecil began shooting at us. She kept us pinned down all day. Every time we would move, she would take a shot at us." Thompson advised his crew to carry rifles, Hancock continued, "It was difficult to work, keep an eye out for Cecil and keep a rifle handy." Often the men returned to the site to find that Cecil had torn down the fence and they had to start all over. "She would shoot at us every day. I'll tell you she kept us scared all the time." Mary May Baily responded to this, "If she wanted to hit the men, she would have, Cecil was a perfect shot."

John Thompson and a few other ranchers repeatedly pushed the authorities to do something. Sherriff Ben Pearson was reluctant to press charges. It was even rumored he had anonymously taken boxes of groceries to Cecil's house knowing she was almost starving and too proud to ask for help.

On March 5, 1954 the noose tightened. Law enforcement and local ranchers arrived at Cecil's home. Evidence of rustling was irrefutable. 21 head of cattle from 5 different ranches were found. She was told she was under arrest.

Deputy Sherriff Jim Brisendine recalled what happened next, "Cecil said, 'Jim, would it be alright if I walked up to the house and used the bathroom?' She had no sooner left when it dawned on me that there was no bathroom in the house. I regretted we had not brought a matron (female deputy) with us. It was one of the biggest mistakes we could have made. A few minutes later we heard a shot and I thought, 'this is it, we will have to shoot her or she will shoot us.' The house remained silent. We walked up to the door and called out several times. Finally I kicked in the door, not sure if I would be looking down the barrel of her rifle. Cecil was dead. Kneeling on the floor she had shot herself with her .30-30 rifle."

The officers and ranchers were stunned at the condition of the home. It was clean and neat as a pin. Lovely blond furniture carefully branded with her Rafter 3 brand decorated the tiny living room. Cecil had painted beautiful paintings that were hung on every wall in oil, water color and chalk. Scenes of the desert, landscapes and pictures of wildlife that looked like a professional and were absolutely fantastic. It was very feminine. A further search revealed manuscripts of poetry and western fiction all written in long hand. Not a penny was found in the house, a bank book showed the account had been closed 4 years earlier. There was no food not even salt or pepper. There was just a pot of beef, rustled, simmering on the back of the wood stove.

Epilogue

When she died on March 5, 1954 she was under arrest for cattle rustling, quite probably the only 20th century cattle rustler in Arizona. Had she been born 50 years earlier she would have gone down in history with the likes of Annie Oakley and Calamity Jane. Cecil's suicide created a sensation in Winslow and back lash of anger which left the officers fearing for their safety. Cecil had left her ranch to the only man she really trusted, her lawyer friend, Dewey McCauley of Winslow. McCauley felt bad about keeping the ranch himself and when a sister, Ruth Moore was located in Ogden, Kansas he turned the ranch over to her in order to keep it in the family. Ruth Moore promptly sold the ranch to Cecil's hated enemy, John Thompson. Vandals began looting around the ranch so all of Cecil's artwork and her manuscripts were taken to a storage unit for safe keeping. Unfortunately, the storage unit caught fire and everything was lost. The only remaining item that belonged to Cecil is a doll that is at the Old Trails Museum in Winslow. John Thompson was "persona non grada" in Winslow, with many blaming him for Cecil's death. In November of 1993, he was found dead of natural causes out on his range.

A doll found in Cecil's home, the only thing left that belonged to her, on display at the Old Trails Museum. Photo courtesy of the archives of the Old Trails Museum/ Winslow Historical Society, www.oldtrailsmuseum.org

Life Facts:
George Creswell 1893-1936
Cecil Creswell 1901-1954

The Rumble Seat
Verner G. Benson
August 1973

The rumble seat has vanished from the scene and I, for one, say 'good riddance to it.' There are those who mourn its passing. Without exception, these are people who, over the intervening years, have thawed out and gotten the dust out of their hair. They mourn a dream, not a reality.

Dust covered magazines, retrieved from attics, still portray advertisements of cars with rumble seats. In these advertisements, the car always rest upon a green lawn. The rumble seat contains a handsome young man and a pretty girl. They are waving, not calling for help, just waving. The young man is bareheaded, his hair neatly combed; the girl is wearing a large hat; both are smiling. In a real rumble seat, at any speed over ten miles an hour, the hat would he snatched from the young lady's head; the young man's hair would look somewhat like a broken bale of straw, and continued smiles would result in a mouthful of dust.

Rumble seats, for the uninitiated, were placed in the turtlebacks of coupes and convertibles. A lid lifted up from the turtleback and, when upholstered with imitation leather and springs, formed the back of a seat. An unbelievably uncomfortable seat was installed inside. It was a narrow seat but could contain two ordinary people or one fat lady and a cat.

Entering a rumble seat was no small matter. A small round step was installed on the left rear bumper. Another round step was installed on the top of the left rear fender. Rumble seats were, obviously, designed for the young, for entering them required the agility of a mountain goat. Leaving them was no easier, and this was further compounded by the fact that two hours exposure to the elements left the occupants stiff and numb. Leg room was inadequate and was further complicated by the presence of jacks, tire chains, rubber boots and empty bottles.

While the rumble seat was no joy to occupy while the car was standing still, it was only when the car was in motion that the full impact could be realized. Here the weatherman's theory of the chilling factor applies. This theory holds that each mile of wind is the equivalent of dropping the temperature one degree. Therefore, riding in a rumble seat at a temperature of 50 degrees, traveling at a speed of sixty miles an hour left the inhabitant shivering at a frosty ten degrees below zero.

Aside from the chilling factor, dust was always a problem. The rumble seat coincided with unpaved roads and roads so narrow, meeting another car involved driving with one wheel in a bar pit. Nor was this ordinary or garden variety dust,

for it contained cinders, small shards of metal, bits of rubber, oil, both hot and cold, stones, and a variety of unidentified objects. Added to this was the dread possibility of thrown objects ancient and venerable eggs, over-ripe fruit, and bags filled with water. Some people just hated a sport. Even on wide paved roads, the rumble seat offered little pleasure, for the wind whipped around the enclosed portion of the car, hats disappeared, ties whipped frantically, and conversation was impossible.

To all this injury was often added insult. One cold January night we became desperate. Our pleas to slow down to ten, not ten M.P.H. but ten below zero, had been ignored. The cold and wind became unbearable.

Searching amid the debris in the rumble seat, we retrieved two pillow-cases. They were quite dirty and had possibly been used to transport boot-leg whiskey, for they contained bits of glass. Gratefully we pulled them over our heads and basked in the delicious warmth.

Our triumph was short lived, however, for a highway patrolman followed us all the way to town. Thought he was breaking up a meeting of the Ku Klux Klan.

Chapter Six

Katherine
Beard
1908-1998

Katherine (right) and her sister Helen, circa 1912. Photo courtesy of Christian Communiciations, Inc. Wichita, KS.

Eight year old Katherine Beard's eyes flew open as she realized it was morning. Was her mother still alive? Katherine jumped out of bed to find out. Leaving slippers and robe behind, she raced down the hall in her nightie and stopped at her parents' bedroom door. Slowly she opened the door and tiptoed to her mother's bedside. Katherine breathed a sigh of relief as her mother opened her eyes and smiled at her.

Kate Beard was beautiful and full of fun before Tuberculosis had ravaged her body. Katherine's father, John Beard was an engineer with the Santa Fe Railroad and was based in the small town of Wellington, Kansas, population 8,000. Kate cared for the three children, Loren, Helen and Katherine as best she could but she tired so easily with the simplest tasks that eventually they had to hire help. Hattie, whose parents had been slaves, was a treasure to the family.

There came a day when Katherine was only 11 that Kate Beard was not alive. Six years later, John Beard died suddenly of a heart attack while driving the train. Katherine finished her last year of high school an orphan. After graduation, Katherine did what most girls did if they pursued college. There were not many options for young women in the 1920's. She enrolled in the state teachers college in Emporia. After one year, Katherine knew she DID NOT want to be a teacher! The tiny inheritance John had left the children was now gone. What Katherine really wanted to do was go to Bible College. She applied and was accepted at Northwestern Bible School in Minneapolis. She did have a pass on the Santa Fe which Katherine would use throughout her life. Katherine loved Bible School! She particularly loved how all the teachers knew the names of every student and really cared about them. "It was right down my alley," she said, "It was never hard for me to complete the assignments or do the homework."

There was a "job finding" program for students who didn't have the funds to pay for school. One of Katherine's favorite professors, Miss Acomb was responsible for the program. Katherine's first job was in the kitchen. She arrived at 4:30am and worked peeling vegetables for lunch and dinner. Bushels of potatoes, carrots and rutabagas. Then she would rush to class and study late into the night.

"Later Miss Acomb sent me out to work as a maid for a wealthy family," Katherine recalled. "This was disastrous. The woman put me in a tiny room with no heat, no place to study, and almost no light to read after dark. She worked me like a slave, and after I had cooked and served a big dinner till late at night, she gave me no food to eat and I was left with all the dishes and the mess to clean up. What was worse, I began to find large welts on my body, and found my little room was infested with bed bugs."

Katherine didn't complain for she was afraid she would lose her job and have to quit college. One day Miss Acomb discovered the welts on Katherine's body and forced the truth out of Katherine. "What the Dean told this woman could have burned the telephone wires!" Katherine said. Miss Acomb demanded that the woman pay Katherine what was owed to her and pay for her to be moved back to the college. Katherine was put into the school dorm until she could recuperate from all she had suffered at the hands of this cruel woman.

However, Katherine was frustrated for she knew she could not afford to live in the dormitory and without a job, she would have to quit school. One morning one of the older students heard her crying. She went in and prayed with Katherine and encouraged her with some scripture verses. Katherine made a covenant with the Lord. She said, "At any cost, at any loss and at any cross I would follow him. I wiped away my tears and went forward with a renewed faith." That very day a wealthy woman called the Dean's Office and said, "I need a nurse maid for just one day. The girl who was caring for my children has quit. The girl will not have to do any other work, we have servants for that. Her whole duty will be caring for the children." Katherine did such a good job that she was hired permanently by Mrs. Hill with time given off for her school work. Her new position was wonderful. She had a lovely room and bath in the section of the house with the family, so she could be close to the two lovely girls age four and two. A maid kept her room and she ate with the children, so her food was the best. She spent her summer with the family at their lake home, where her total responsibility was the children. "I could sit on the beach and watch the children as they paddled about in the water. I enjoyed every minute of those days at the lake."

One of Katherine's favorite activities was listening to missionaries. She was especially drawn to those working with the Indians. "As I began learning about the American Indians, of their history and the tragedies of mistreatment by the early American people I began to labor under a great burden for them. God put a love for them in my heart, though I knew no Indians and couldn't tell one tribe from another."

At a church service, Katherine was intrigued by a Hopi man who encouraged her, "Come out to Hopi-Navajo land and help us" Katherine again used her Santa Fe Railroad pass, and boarded a train to Winslow, Arizona.

In December of 1932 Katherine arrived to begin missionary work full of hopes and dreams. What happened next would be a nightmare that lasted a full year. Harvey, (not his real name) was there to meet her at the train along with a young man he identified as his son. Katherine was taken to a pickup truck and her foot locker and suitcase tossed into the back. This was a new experience as she had never ridden in a truck before. The pickup started north and soon they ran out of paved road and were bumping along on a dirt road. Very little was said during the day as they drove along further and further from civilization. The man and his son talked in Hopi and did not translate. "We saw nothing but barren land and the further we went the more we saw of nothing, just miles and miles of barrenness." Finally, late in the afternoon they passed what Katherine was to learn was a deserted Navajo hogan. Harvey stopped the truck, got Katherine's suitcase and foot locker out and said, "Well, here is where you get out. This will be your home: from here you can begin your mission work to the Indians." Then they got into the pickup and roared away.

Katherine said, "I came out of the hogan and looked around. Here I was a million miles from nowhere, or so it seemed. I went back into my new home an looked around. This was the first time I had seen a round house. I had never been in one made of mud and dirt either. I found the roof was made of logs put together in crisscross fashion and mudded over. The walls were also made of logs and covered with mud. The floor of course was dirt. There was only one small low doorway – there was no door. There was no furniture, not even a stove. In the center I could see a pile of ashes which told me this is where the fire was located and looking up I saw a hole in the roof, thourough which I could see blue sky above. This must be for the smoke to go out. There was dead rabbit lying near the ashes and a pair of worn out shoes." Katherine stood alone in the hogan in shock. Why had Harvey done this to her? It was growing cold as evening came one. How could she keep warm? There was no wood. Where was the nearest house? It would do no good to shout or cry, there was no one to hear her. "All of a sudden I realized I was not alone! The Lord was with me why should I need any human being? My situation was impossible, but God can do things with the impossible. I remembered my covenant with the Lord, 'At any cost and any loss at any cross I will follow you', Did I really mean that?" So then I said, "It's all right Lord, the next move is yours." Right there and then I had a wonderful prayer and praise time in that old hogan. A peace came over me and I knew God was in control."

Not long afterward Katherine heard the sound of the pickup truck. It turned out to be Harvey. He was very disappointed that Katherine was cool as a cucumber. Riding along through the night Katherine wondered what kind of man she had come to work with. Little did she realize that he had invited her to Arizona for only one reason. It was his intent to seduce Katherine and use her for his own immoral purposes. Little did Harvey realize that this tiny women, no more than 5 feet tall, no more than 100 pounds was all steel inside and would be more than a match for his evil desires. He was not a missionary, and certainly not a Christian. He was a wealthy man; he had large flocks of sheep and cattle. He had a job with the tribal agency and was postmaster of the local post office. He was a predator, and Katherine was not his first victim.

As they bumped along through the night they came to another hogan, but this one was occupied. "After waiting a few minutes, the men got out and told me to follow, as they pulled back the blanket on the hogan door. Inside sat a dear elderly couple. We three sat down on the blanket they had spread for us. In a moment the old grandfather came over and clasped each of our hands. Then his wife came and did the same. Then Harvey stated his business. This couple was caring for some of his sheep. Soon all the men left and grandmother and I were alone. Grandmother could not speak a word of English and I knew no Navajo, yet we were very comfortable together. We conversed with our smiles and our actions. We were saying, 'I love you! I trust you!' She had coffee on the fire and soon began to make fry bread, I had never smelled anything so delicious and I was so hungry for it had been a long day."

Again they drove on through the night; Katherine was so weary she didn't know how much longer it took. Finally they arrived in Pollaca. There were only a few lights shining out from a few houses. A tired and very bewildered Katherine Beard stepped out to begin her life among the Hopi Indians. Katherine was amazed the next morning to find she was high a top a mesa. The village was built in pueblo style with the houses built right next to each other. The mesa was narrow, only about 200 feet across but 1,000 feet in length. Flat as a pancake the edge dropped down hundreds of feet to the valley below, she could see for miles and miles in every direction. Harvey didn't live in one of the typical pueblo homes, but in a separate house with four rooms.

Along with Harvey lived his second wife, a white woman who was a registed nurse, who lived in fear of him. There were three children from his first marriage and the woman stayed on for their sakes for she loved them. There was also a widowed missionary named Iva living there. She had planned to leave but when she heard about Katherine she stayed on to protect the young missionary who apparently had fallen prey to Harvey.

Harvey did everything in his power to seduce Katherine. He moved the desk into the bedroom and tried to get Katherine to work with him in there. She refused to be alone with him. "If you want to dictate a letter to me you can do it right here on the kitchen table." He wanted to take her places, she refused. "Sometimes I just had to tell him off something awful. I was never afraid to speak up to him. I let him know I would have nothing to do with a man of his sort. I was never sorry I was so hard on him. He found out he couldn't do anything with me. No one else in the house dared speak up to him, but I developed a holy boldness and would let him have it in no uncertain terms."

Harvey tried many approaches. He offered to buy her jewelry. She told him she didn't want any. He offered to build her a stone house. She refused. He offered to take her to the Grand Canyon to see the all the sights. She laughed. "You could have so much fun," said Harvey. Katherine replied, "I don't want your kind of fun."

However when Katherine threatened to leave and go back to Winslow, he told her it was 80 miles and she had no way to go. She told him she would ride on the mail truck which came out three times a week, but since Harvey was the Post-master, he had the power to prohibit her. So there she was, a virtual prisoner at Pollaca.

Harvey did have to go to work and Katherine had that time to begin a work with the Hopi children. She recalled, "The Hopi children were delightful. The children would come running when they saw me. They could run so fast it would terrify me that they would fall over the cliff, but they would stop just in time. Most of them could speak English and they loved the Bible stories and the little games we played." Katherine discovered Hopi's love for music, both singing and instrumental. Before long there was a "Hopi Band" in action. The band consisted of all men but the director was a woman, ---Katherine with her violin.

Katherine said, "I wanted so much to get back to the Navajo hogan where that dear old grandmother welcomed me and showed such kindness to me. Finally one day when I knew Harvey was gone for the day I borrowed a horse, put my Bible and some quilt blocks in a bag and started out. I found a Navajo man who was willing to go and translate. When I arrived at any Navajo hogan, I always took the time to get to know them. I would first talk about their home, their children, their crops and their horses. I would ask, 'How many sheep do you have? How are the sheep doing?' Many questions like that, they were so happy I was interested in their lives. And the quilt blocks were a real attraction for always they are in need warm coverings for their beds which are just a blanket or a sheepskin on the floor. I waited for the Lord to guide me to begin to talk about 'The God who sits in heaven and the Good News.' The people were always thrilled to hear the Good News! They were tired of the medicine men. They hold the people in bondage by filling them with fears and they bleed the people for any money, any sheep, any horses anything they have. The medicine men will do nothing for the people unless they pay and pay dearly."

"When Harvey found out I had gone out visiting, he was

furious." Katherine recalled, "Finally Iva suggested we try to get away. We knew a missionary couple, the Stokelys, working with the Navajos. Iva secretly got a letter off to the Stokelys telling of their plight and when Harvey would not be at home." The plan worked and soon Mr. Stokely was knocking at the door and said to Harvey's wife, "I have come for the two Anglo women who are here." The wife did not protest and Iva and Katherine quickly gathered their belongings which were packed and ready to go. After one long year Katherine was free at last.

Katherine with two lambs from a Navajo family's flock, circa 1930's. Photo courtesy of Christian Communiciations, Inc. Wichita, KS.

For a time Katherine lived with the Stokelys. It was during this time that she met Bruce. Katherine tells the fascinating story of his life. "In the early days of the Navajos they frequently raided other tribes, and also down into Mexico. On one raid they stole a Mexican boy who grew up to be a Navajo medicine man. He married a woman from the Jemez Indian tribe and soon they had a son who they named Bruce. This boy was half Mexican and half Jemez but he lived among the Navajos, so he grew up Navajo and was fluent in the Navajo language. He also spoke English. Bruce was one of the first converts and he soon became a great helper to them since he was a very good interpreter."

"Bruce and I had a lot of fun together. He had a real sense of humor and liked to play tricks on me. He would tie a mouse to the doorknob just to hear me scream. Sometimes we would be out visiting and we would get lost. Bruce would laugh and say, 'White man lost, but Indian not lost. Indian find the way'. Then he would be off like a streak and run ahead. Finally he would come back and tell us which way to go. Many times we looked to Bruce to find the way home, especially after the wind had wiped out the tracks we had made. Bruce always got us home."

"Bruce and I shared a coal shed at the Stokely's. It had no heat and no water. All I had in my room was a bed, a stand and a kerosene lamp. I kept all my clothes in a foot locker. In the evening, I would sit on my bed and practice my violin, or read my Bible or play my auto harp and watch the rats run around. For some reason I wasn't afraid of them and I am sure they ran all over the bed at night."

For five years the Stokely's tried to get some land from the Navajo authorities. Katherine describes what happened, "One day we heard there would be a meeting and we were to attend. We went to the appointed place and met with a large number of Navajos and many policemen, who were all mounted on horses. There was lots of talk, most of it we couldn't understand. Then everything got quiet and their leader stepped forward. He was a large man and very old. He lifted his arms and said to the people, 'Come on my children. We want the missionaries to live among us!' Every Navajo there stood up and voted to let us have the property. The Navajos granted us 5 acres of land 16 miles north of Orabi, called Hard Rock." Mission work continues there to this day, under the direction of Navajo leadership.

Katherine was called upon to perform many duties. Rattlesnakes were thought to be demons so the people were very frightened. More than once, Katherine armed with a club entered a strange hogan to face an angry rattler and club it to death.

This same fear of demons was true when death came to the hogan. Katherine tells of many hogans with nothing in them but the bones of the person who died there. Many deaths were caused by tuberculosis, the same disease that had claimed Katherine's mother. She treated and cleaned many a TB patient, yet miraculously never contracted the disease. Tuberculosis was a frightful scourge among the Navajo and Hopi people. Katherine explained the fear of death and demons. "They would care for the person until they heard the death rattle in the throat. Then they would pick up the blanket on which the person lay, one person at each end and carry him out to the wilderness as far as they could. There they left him to die alone." Katherine was often called upon to be mortician and funeral director. They heard she was not afraid of the demons because she had a "black book" which was stronger medicine than what the medicine men had. "I have buried many people," Katherine said. "Most of the time Bruce would do the digging, but I often took a turn at the shovel. We had to dig at least 5 feet down because the coyotes would find a shallow grave and dig it up and eat the body."

One time Katherine and Bruce were called upon by a Navajo woman to bury her brother. She described where they had left him. Katherine and Bruce started out and sure enough found him right where the woman said he would be. Bruce started digging the grave and Katherine went closer to get a look at the body. Then he moved! She called out, "Bruce, come here, this fellow is not dead yet, maybe you can still talk to him." Bruce got down on the ground and shouted in the man's ear. "What god do you pray to?" The man mumbled, "I don't know a god to pray to, I just pray to earth" Bruce began to give the man a simple message telling him about God, creation, heaven, and Jesus the son of God who came to take away his sins. The man nodded throughout and they knew he understood. Then the man said he believed in Jesus and called upon Jesus to take away his sins. He was still for a few minutes then said in a clear voice, "I see Heaven! It is a beautiful place. I want to go there."

Another terrible fear relates to twin babies*. Having twins was considered a bad omen to a Navajo family as they believe the second baby was a demon. It was the custom with twins to leave the second baby out in the cold to die or kill it in some way. Katherine was always alert to this situation. Once she and a nurse were visiting where twins had just been born. She asked if they could have the second baby. "The father picked it up and laid it in my lap so fast it surprised me."

The baby, named Benjamin, only 3 pounds went home with them and with good care lived and became a beautiful boy. Many

*My Navajo friends who proofread this story had not heard that twins were a bad omen. This belief may have been confined to a small isolated portion of the reservation. It is also possible that it was introduced by an outsider living in the area.

Navajos came from miles around to see the baby for they had all heard about the little demon baby the missionaries had.

Another baby was about to be thrown over a cliff when he was rescued. His mother had died in childbirth and so it was thought that the baby was to blame and must be killed. They named this baby Daniel. Both of these boys grew up to be strong men and strong Christians. As people saw the children were completely normal, the infanticide disappeared.

One day, a very young girl named Augusta came running to Katherine's little house. She was breathless and heartbroken. She explained that her family had sold her to a very old medicine man that already had many wives. Please help me she said, "I don't want to marry that old man!" Katherine sprang into action, not thinking of the consequences. "I put the girl in the car and drove her 60 miles to the government school. I left her there and was returning home when on a one track road I met the medicine man who was out looking for Augusta. He said I had stolen his girl and wanted to know where I had taken her. Then he said, 'Get out of my way so I can go down the road.' I told him, 'You're a man, you get out of MY way!' We were all alone out there and I guess he could have killed me, but I waited and he finally turned his car around and I went by."

A number of people came to see Katherine about this but she told them she would only talk to the parents. Finally the parents came. It turned out it was the grandmother who had sold Augusta and she was very angry now that she had lost the money. Katherine said, 'I took the girl down to Washington' Navajos called all government agencies Washington. The family made the trip to the boarding school but Augusta did not want to leave, so they left empty handed and Augusta remained at school.

Not surprisingly, after 10 years of working 12-14 hour days, insufficient rest, inadequate diet and a variety of illnesses, Katherine's health broke. She reluctantly returned by train, again using her rail pass to get to Kansas. There she spent time regaining her strength and undergoing a few surgeries. During that time she met Imo Wardlow and recruited her for the work in Arizona.

Katherine decided life on the reservation was too exhausting for now and would set up a base in Flagstaff where life would be easier and there was easy access to medical treatment. Then, if her health improved, maybe she would again be able to move full time to the reservation.

When Katherine and Imo arrived in Flagstaff they were shocked to see a huge number of Indians. "You just couldn't believe it. There were Indians coming into this town like you never saw. You would have thought that all the Navajos, Hopis and Zunis from all over Arizona, Utah, New Mexico and Colorado were in Flagstaff. It was an experience for me to not have to drive miles and miles to find two or three Indians!"

Imo Warldow and Katherine Beard wearing gifts from their Navajo friends, seated in front of a hogan, circa 1950. Photo courtesy of Christian Communiciations, Inc. Wichita, KS.

This was the early days of World War II and men from many tribes were enlisting in the military to fight for their country. Some were there to enlist in the Army, or to be part of the new Navajo Code Talkers. But the main reason so many Indians were in Flagstaff was the huge Army Ammunition Depot 15 miles west of Flagstaff. The Sixth Army had moved in and set up one of the largest facilities in the nation for the storing of ammunition. The facility was called Bellemont. The Army used Indian labor to work at the depot and had constructed Indian villages where the families could live. Katherine described it this way. "There was row upon row of little houses with about 140 families living in them. When I say 'families' I do mean families, for the Indians brought the mothers the fathers, the grandmothers and grandfathers, the uncles and the aunts, children and grandchildren, blood relatives and clan relatives. Actually there was an estimated 1,500 Indians living at Bellemont at that time."

Katherine and Imo started driving out to Bellemont every day, regardless of the weather. Soon they found out that they could not enter without passing through several guard stations and a lot of red tape. Katherine said, "You almost had to sign your life away to get into the place. And this happened every time we went to Bellemont." She added, "We decided to do something about it. We had noticed that the Army had built a little chapel on the Depot for the white workers. But there was no chapel or any provision for the spiritual needs of the Indians living on the base. This is typical of the government. We mustered up our courage and asked if we could see Colonel Custis who was in charge of the Depot. We were pushed from one guard to the next, one secretary to the next but finally we entered the office of Colonel Custis. Colonel Custis stood when they entered and asked, 'What can I do for you ladies?' This seemed like a good beginning so we told him what we wanted. Within two weeks we received a formal letter from Colonel Custis saying that he would make us the authorized protestant missionaries to do religious work among the Navajos and Hopis at Bellemont!"

Every day the ladies would pack a lunch and drive out to Bellemont. The Colonel gave them a pass so the guards waved them through. Katherine said, "We would spend 12-14 hours a day visiting with the Indians in their homes. We found the people, both Navajo and Hopi with open hearts to us and to the Gospel. Our first convert was a Navajo woman who was seated on the floor weaving a Navajo rug. Her heart was very tender. She eagerly listened to the Good News we shared from the Bible and she was ready to commit to Jesus, regardless of the cost to her."

"When the Colonel saw how much good we were doing for the Indians he seemed willing to give us anything we asked. We needed a place to begin holding meetings so he offered us the school building. In addition to visiting, and holding meetings, we began running a full scale Sunday school for the children and started both Boy Scouts and Girl Scouts." Katherine summed up her time in Bellemont saying, "Through the years, thousands of people found Jesus and today throughout the southwest on many reservations one can find Indian Christians who will

The little schoolhouse at the Gap, AZ, where Katherine conducted Gospel meetings. Photo courtesy of Christian Communiciations, Inc. Wichita, KS.

tell you they found the Lord at the Bellemont Church."

Activities at the Depot continued for many years, all through World War 11 and then at a slower pace after the war ended. When the Korean War broke out, the Depot operated again at full capacity.

Many things happened in the forties and fifties. Katherine eventually established her own mission, based in Flagstaff, which she called, Flagstaff Mission to the Navajos. A number of churches were started which remain today pastored by Navajo Christian men. One of the men, Leslie Cody and his wife Rose Mary, remembered her in this way. "We knew Miss Beard loved the people and she was so kind. You could see she loved the Lord. She was always interested in every person she met, and she would pray for you, and do all kinds of things for you. The people really love her and she gets along with them in a wonderful way."

She continued working well into her 80's. Finally at the age of 93 she moved to Sedona to the Kachina Point health care facility where she lived for

Katherine visiting a friend in a Navajo hogan. Photo courtesy of Christian Communiciations, Inc. Wichita, KS.

5 years until her death in 1998. Katherine had worked tirelessly but had never taken much income. This nice facility was paid for through friends and descendants of her brother and sister, Loren and Helen.

Epilogue

I remember Miss Beard back in the 70's and 80's. Everyone, including Imo Wardlow called her Miss Beard. I was in awe of her. After reading the book by Hart Armstrong that had been written about her and from which most of this story came I was even more in awe! I can barely lift a 50 pound bag of dog food, how in the world did she move bodies and bury them? How did she persevere after that horrible year in Pollaca? Most people would have run home and never returned. I did wonder how Navajos felt about her now. I know many Navajos at my church, Flagstaff Christian Fellowship, so I began to ask them. Katherine Beard is still remembered decades later with love, respect and admiration. Jamie Esplain said, "Her help was very welcome in the physical realm, but more importantly her spiritual help made a lasting impact on my people." Vernon and Gwen Cody said, "She is respected all across the Navajo Nation."

Life Facts:
Katherine Ruth Beard, May 7, 1908- April 21,1998

Navajo Name: Asdzan Yazzie, which means "Little Lady". They often added "Little Lady-with-the-black-book" or "Little Lady-who-says-she-is-sorry" because when the Navajos would tell her of a difficulty or tragedy, she would always say, "Oh, I am so sorry!"

Favorite quote: "At any cost, at any loss, and at any cross I will follow you."

Favorite recipe: Fry Bread

Acknowledgements

Sarah Ashurst
Thanks to my friend, Everett Ashurst for all the wonderful stories of his great-grandmother, Sarah. Everett continues the Ashurst ranching tradition in Southeastern Arizona as well as pastoring a church. Thanks also to Ed Ashurst, grandson of Sarah for his remembrance of his grandmother. Thanks to Randon Cupp and Michael Higdon for their help in determining the value of the 10,000 poker win. Books: Ashurst, Henry F. A Many Colored Toga University of Arizona Press 1962   Cline, Platt They Came to the Mountain Northern Arizona University with Northland Press Flagstaff, Arizona 1976.

Kate Lyall
Thanks to Dave and Barbara Penny for their remembrance of Barbara's great grandmother Kate. Thanks to Dale Lyall for providing pictures and written personal accounts. Thanks for the wonderful conversations about Kate at Brandy's in Flagstaff plus some fantastic grandparenting tips from the experts!

Martha Purtymun
Thanks to Paul Thompson, grandson of Oak Creeks first settler, Jim Thompson. Paul's personal remembrance of "Grandma Cook" and all the early pioneer families in Oak Creek Canyon and Sedona is of great interest and tremendous help for all my books! Thanks to Janeen Trevillyan and the Sedona Historical Society/ Sedona Heritage Museum for use of their archives/research facility, photos and additional information. This museum is a MUST for locals and visitors alike! Books: McBride, Laura Purtyman. Traveling by Tin Lizzie: The Great Model-T Road Trip of 1924 Pronto Press Sedona, Arizona 1980.

Guadalupe Vasquez
Thanks to Mary Vasquez Powell and her husband Kent for the family photos and their warm remembrance of Mary's grandparents, Guadalupe and Tranquilino Vasquez. Every meeting was delightful!

Cecil Creswell
Thanks to the staff of Old Trails Museum who gave me the article about Cecil Creswell. After reading her story I knew I had to include it in the next book.   Thanks to Ann-Mary J. Lutzick for all her help in getting more information about Cecil and providing me with pictures. (The archives of the Old Trails Museum/Winslow Historical Society, www.oldtrailsmuseum.org)

Thanks to Randy Hummel, lifelong Winslow resident for his knowledge and additional information about Cecil. Article: Thomas, Bob. "The Astonishing Double Life of Frontier Rancher Cecil Creswell." Arizona Highways, October 1995.

Katherine Beard
Thanks to my friend, Charlene Talbott who handed me a book at church one day and said, "This would make a good story for your next book" Thanks to Beth Ann Hardin of Wichita, Kansas for granting permission for photos in the book. Thanks to my Navajo friends who proofed for cultural accuracy, Jamie Esplain, Betty Russell and Vernon and Gwen Cody. Thanks to my friend Jane Scott for driving me all over the reservation, Pollaca, Hoteveilla and Chinle to see where both Katherine and Cecil Creswell had lived. Book: Armstrong, Hart. "A Life Poured Out." Christian Communications. Wichita, Kansas. 1988.

Thanks to my proof readers, Cathy Arminio, Charlene Talbott, and Lisa Wilcox. Thanks to my daughter, Lisa Blalock, for not only proofing the stories, but her great encouragement and helpful suggestions.

Thanks again to my Dad for writing stories that just get better with time! The stories in this book contain some of my favorites.

Thanks to Stephanie Goodwin for transcribing all of my dad's original stories onto the computer.

Thanks to Joe Meehan, director of Pioneer Museum and Riordan Mansion State Park here in Flagstaff. Joe is always so helpful and knowledgeable about all things Northern Arizona. Flagstaff's two historical museums, The Pioneer Museum on Fort Valley Road and Riordan Mansion State Park are also a MUST for locals and visitors.

Thanks to my own Flagstaff Public Library for creating the most pleasant working environment. All the stories were written there and the staff was always so helpful with finding information, books, and helping me repeatedly to use the microfilm and access census records and genology for all the stories.

Thanks to Randi Diskin for her amazing work in putting this all together and voila, it's a book!